Become a KS3 English genius — with CGP!

This CGP book is packed with a whole year's worth of 10-Minute Workouts — perfect for practising Year 9 English in short, regular bursts.

Every workout covers Reading, Writing and SPaG skills, with a variety of texts to put you to the test. Plus, there's one for each week of the school year — wow!

Answers are included at the back, along with a handy score sheet to track your progress throughout the year. Trust us to have everything sorted!

A note for teachers, parents and caregivers

Just something to bear in mind if you're choosing further reading for Year 9 pupils — all the extracts in this book are suitable for children of this age, but we can't vouch for the full texts they're taken from, or other works by the same authors.

Published by CGP
ISBN: 978 1 83774 050 5

Editors: Claire Boulter, Heather Cowley, Robbie Driscoll, Rebecca Greaves, Nathan Mair, James Summersgill

With thanks to Kirsty Sweetman and John Sanders for the proofreading.

With thanks to Jade Sim for the copyright research.

Clipart from Corel®

Printed by Zenith Print & Packaging Ltd, Pontypridd.
Based on the classic CGP style created by Richard Parsons.

Text, design, layout and original illustrations
© Coordination Group Publications Ltd. (CGP) 2023
All rights reserved.

Photocopying this book is not permitted, even if you have a CLA licence.
Extra copies are available from CGP with next day delivery • 0800 1712 712 • www.cgpbooks.co.uk

How to Use this Book

- This book contains 36 workouts. We've split them into 3 sections — one for each term, with 12 workouts each. There's roughly one workout for every week of the school year.

- Each workout is out of 12 marks and should take about 10 minutes to complete.

- The workouts start with a short warm-up question, followed by a text with some reading questions. Pupils then move on to a spelling, punctuation or grammar question and finish with some writing skills practice.

- The workouts progress in difficulty, so they're perfect for ensuring that pupils are getting to grips with Year 9 English.

- Answers, a glossary and a score sheet can be found at the back of the book.

The contents page for each term shows you the main reading and writing skills and text types covered in each workout.

Some of these topics are then retested in the following terms at a slightly higher level to provide more practice.

Each workout also tests a different spelling, punctuation or grammar skill, providing practice of a range of topics across the book.

The workouts in each term can be done in any order — pick the one that best suits the needs of your pupils.

The tick boxes on the contents pages can help you to keep a record of which workouts have been attempted.

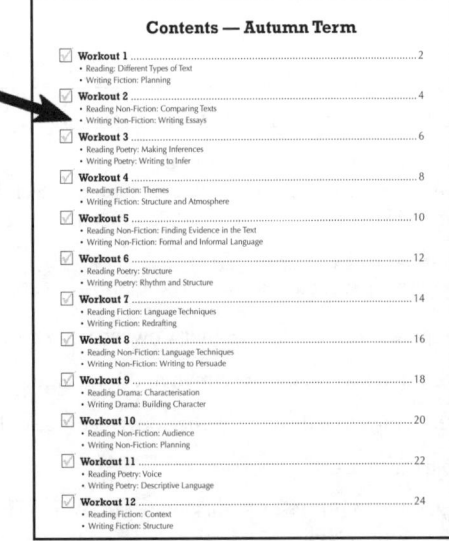

Contents — Autumn Term

- [ ] **Workout 1** 2
  - Reading: Different Types of Text
  - Writing Fiction: Planning
- [ ] **Workout 2** 4
  - Reading Non-Fiction: Comparing Texts
  - Writing Non-Fiction: Writing Essays
- [ ] **Workout 3** 6
  - Reading Poetry: Making Inferences
  - Writing Poetry: Writing to Infer
- [ ] **Workout 4** 8
  - Reading Fiction: Themes
  - Writing Fiction: Structure and Atmosphere
- [ ] **Workout 5** 10
  - Reading Non-Fiction: Finding Evidence in the Text
  - Writing Non-Fiction: Formal and Informal Language
- [ ] **Workout 6** 12
  - Reading Poetry: Structure
  - Writing Poetry: Rhythm and Structure
- [ ] **Workout 7** 14
  - Reading Fiction: Language Techniques
  - Writing Fiction: Redrafting
- [ ] **Workout 8** 16
  - Reading Non-Fiction: Language Techniques
  - Writing Non-Fiction: Writing to Persuade
- [ ] **Workout 9** 18
  - Reading Drama: Characterisation
  - Writing Drama: Building Character
- [ ] **Workout 10** 20
  - Reading Non-Fiction: Audience
  - Writing Non-Fiction: Planning
- [ ] **Workout 11** 22
  - Reading Poetry: Voice
  - Writing Poetry: Descriptive Language
- [ ] **Workout 12** 24
  - Reading Fiction: Context
  - Writing Fiction: Structure

Contents — Spring Term

- [ ] **Workout 1** 26
    - Reading Non-Fiction: Writer's Intention
    - Writing Non-Fiction: Writing to Advise
- [ ] **Workout 2** 28
    - Reading Fiction: Making Inferences
    - Writing Fiction: Redrafting and Proofreading
- [ ] **Workout 3** 30
    - Reading Non-Fiction: Purpose
    - Writing Non-Fiction: Writing to Inform, Explain and Advise
- [ ] **Workout 4** 32
    - Reading Poetry: Comparing Poems
    - Writing Poetry: Rhythm, Rhyme and Descriptive Language
- [ ] **Workout 5** 34
    - Reading Fiction: What You Think
    - Writing Fiction: Quoting
- [ ] **Workout 6** 36
    - Reading Non-Fiction: Tone
    - Writing Non-Fiction: Redrafting and Proofreading
- [ ] **Workout 7** 38
    - Reading Drama: Staging and Performance
    - Writing Drama: Play Scripts
- [ ] **Workout 8** 40
    - Reading Non-Fiction: Layout and Structure
    - Writing Non-Fiction: Writing Essays
- [ ] **Workout 9** 42
    - Reading Poetry: Techniques
    - Writing Poetry: Descriptive Language
- [ ] **Workout 10** 44
    - Reading Fiction: Understanding Setting
    - Writing Fiction: Building Setting
- [ ] **Workout 11** 46
    - Reading Non-Fiction: Language Techniques
    - Writing Non-Fiction: Writing to Persuade
- [ ] **Workout 12** 48
    - Reading Fiction: Language Techniques
    - Writing Fiction: Figurative Language

Contents — Summer Term

☑ **Workout 1** 50
- Reading Non-Fiction: Tone
- Writing Non-Fiction: Redrafting and Proofreading

☑ **Workout 2** 52
- Reading Poetry: Interpreting Poems
- Writing Poetry: Grammar

☑ **Workout 3** 54
- Reading Fiction: Characterisation
- Writing Fiction: Quoting

☑ **Workout 4** 56
- Reading Non-Fiction: Making Inferences
- Writing Non-Fiction: Writing Essays

☑ **Workout 5** 58
- Reading Fiction: Comparing Texts
- Writing Fiction: Writing Stories

☑ **Workout 6** 60
- Reading Non-Fiction: Writer's Intention
- Writing Non-Fiction: Structure

☑ **Workout 7** 62
- Reading Poetry: Themes
- Writing Poetry: Language Techniques

☑ **Workout 8** 64
- Reading Fiction: Structure
- Writing Fiction: Writing Stories

☑ **Workout 9** 66
- Reading Non-Fiction: What You Think
- Writing Non-Fiction: Redrafting and Proofreading

☑ **Workout 10** 68
- Reading Drama: Interpreting Plays
- Writing Drama: Play Scripts

☑ **Workout 11** 70
- Reading Non-Fiction: Layout and Structure
- Writing Non-Fiction: Writing Essays

☑ **Workout 12** 72
- Reading Poetry: Comparing Poems
- Writing Poetry: Language Techniques

Answers 74

Glossary & Score Sheet 83

Autumn Term: Workout 1

Warm up

1. Write either 'brought' or 'bought' in the gaps. Use each word once.

    We .... back some sweets that we .... on holiday.

    (1 mark)

Reading Questions

A Surely all of us gathered here today agree that banning costumes on the charity ski race is absurd. Isn't it supposed to be a bit of fun? The crowd always love it! Think of all the cheers, the laughs and, not least, the donations that costumes bring.

B Are you in need of an ultra-balanced snowboard? Look no further — the LevelUpp is perfect for you. With its glossy exterior, adjustable flexibility and, most importantly, its fall-proof technology, riders of this board will never find themselves sprawled in the snow. Call now to order!

C Surrounded by silent snowfall, Cleo headed down the slope, hearing only the hush of her skis in the snow and the whisper of the wind in the trees. Carving a path through the freshly fallen layer, she felt like the world was hers alone.

2. What type of text do you think each extract above is from?

    a) ....   b) ....   c) ....

    (1 mark)

3. a) Name a technique that is used in both Text A and Text B.

    ....

    b) Why do you think the writers of these texts have used this technique?

    ....

    (2 marks)

4. What effect does the use of onomatopoeia in Text C have on the reader?

    ....

    (1 mark)

Spelling, Punctuation & Grammar Question

5. Complete each word by adding either 'cious' or 'tious'.

    a) Our gra............ hosts at the chalet offered us a nutri............ breakfast.

    b) Tackling that slope is ambi............ — my last attempt was atro............ .

    (2 marks)

Writing Question

6. Below is a brief plan for a short story. Rewrite the plan, adding extra detail to each section to make it more useful.

    - Lost snowboarder needs to find a way down mountain.
    - Something bad happens so he has to go somewhere.
    - Snowboarder meets some kind of beast.
    - Snowboarder and beast talk.
    - Snowboarder somehow gets down mountain.

Opening	....
1st paragraph	....
2nd paragraph	....
3rd paragraph	....
Ending	....

(5 marks)

Score: ☐ /12

Autumn Term: Workout 2

Warm up

1. Underline the key words or phrases in the following essay question:

   How does the writer use figurative language to describe the city's appearance?

   (1 mark)

Reading Questions

A **Drabston, More Like 'Fabston'**

Five years ago, I found myself in Drabston, a dilapidated, dreary town. Fast-forward to the present day and that same town is thriving. With its refurbished castle, brand-new shopping district (where you can buy everything under the sun) and an entertainment centre boasting an array of family-friendly attractions, you'll never be bored. Who would want to miss out on this town now?

B Several years ago, living in Drabston was a dream. Us locals lived quiet lives, enjoying the beauty, charm and tranquillity of the surrounding countryside, which has since been defaced in the name of 'progress'. Fifty percent of the town's green spaces have been converted to visitor car parks, and even our view of the night sky has been obliterated by the entertainment centre's ghastly fluorescent lights.

2. a) Summarise how the writer of Text A feels about the past version of Drabston.

   ....

   b) Summarise how the writer of Text B feels about the past version of Drabston.

   ....
   (2 marks)

3. Compare the way that each writer uses persuasive language techniques.

   ....

   ....

   ....
   (2 marks)

Spelling, Punctuation & Grammar Question

4. Here is another extract from Text B. Underline the four incorrectly spelt words, then write the correct spelling above it.

> Drabston was supposed to be a tempory home, but after visiting one Wensday, my dad decided to move here permenently and sined a contract to buy a house.

(2 marks)

Writing Question

5. Read the following essay prompt:

> 'Living in a large town or city is better than living in a small village.' Do you agree?

a) Write a sentence explaining each of the three main points you would cover.

Point 1 ....

....

Point 2 ....

....

Point 3 ....

....

(3 marks)

b) Write a short introduction to the essay, in which you outline your argument.

....

....

....

....

(2 marks)

Score: / 12

Autumn Term: Workout 3

Warm up

1. Words have connotations. What is meant by a connotation?

   ....
   (1 mark)

Reading Questions

> *The Flower Garden*
>
> *The old lady down the road*
> *Had a garden full of flowers.*
> *Roses, violets, marigolds —*
> *She'd tend to them for hours.*
> *Each person passing by her house,*
> *Whether a stranger or a friend,*
> *Was gifted a fragrant bouquet;*
> *The blossoms, they'd commend.*
>
> *But soon the townsfolk started*
> *To pick her flowers on their own.*
> *"She'd give them to us anyway,"*
> *They'd hiss and hurry home.*
> *To stop her garden going bare,*
> *She had just one defence.*
> *Now her garden sits behind*
> *A giant wooden fence.*

2. How does the lady feel about her flowers? Give evidence to support your answer.

   ....

   ....
   (2 marks)

3. What does "They'd hiss and hurry home" suggest about the townsfolk?

   ....

   ....
   (1 mark)

4. What do you think is the main message of the poem? Explain your answer.

   ....

   ....
   (2 marks)

Spelling, Punctuation & Grammar Question

5. Here is another poem. Complete each line with the '-ing' form of the verb in brackets.

(Fall) .... leaves spiral down,   Every year sees them (change) ....

Nature (die) .... all around.   Animals start (ready) .... dens,

All the plants slowly (age) ...., (Hope) .... for spring again.

(2 marks)

Writing Questions

6. Rewrite each sentence so that the character's feelings are implied through their behaviour or body language.

   a) Mei was feeling relaxed.

   ....

   b) Rohan was feeling very worried.

   ....

   (2 marks)

7. Write four lines of poetry about a gardener discovering an unusual species of flower. Use language so that the reader has to work out what your character is feeling from the way they are described.

   ....

   ....

   ....

   ....

   (2 marks)

Score: ☐ / 12

Autumn Term: Workout 4

Warm up

1. Generally, you should avoid using clichés when writing a story. Why is this?

   ....

   (1 mark)

Reading Questions

> The window blinds bar my view of the hills, their shadows extending in long streaks over my desk and across my skin. I stifle a sigh, trying to rein my mind back in to focus on my biology test, but all it takes is one lapse in concentration and my thoughts have run off again, taking me through sunlit fields and wildflower meadows, up stony ridges and down deep gorges, along well-worn paths and off the beaten track, where there are no footprints to follow.
>
> And then I'm back in the classroom. Door shut, air stuffy. My blazer is too warm. My tie is too tight. My school shoes pinch my toes; my running shoes don't. I take a deep breath — I need more space in my chest — and try to momentarily forget about the places where I don't have bars on my skin.

2. a) What do you think is the main theme explored in this extract?

    ....

    b) Explain your answer using at least one quote from the extract.

    ....

    ....

    (3 marks)

3. Why do you think the writer uses short sentences in the second paragraph?

    ....

    ....

    (1 mark)

Spelling, Punctuation & Grammar Question

4. Circle the correct spelling to complete each sentence below.

   a) I'm **desperate / desparate** to go outside — it's such nice weather today!

   b) Efia is a **voluntry / voluntary** marshal during running events.

   c) If I go on a run without a coat, it's **definately / definitely** going to rain.

   (3 marks)

Writing Question

5. Imagine that you've been asked to write a story about a character who is participating in a running race, but during the race, things keep going wrong.

   a) Write an opening to the story that grabs the reader's attention.

   ....
   ....
   ....
   ....

   (2 marks)

   b) Write a plan for the rest of the story. Mention the atmosphere you want to create, and how you will structure your story to maintain the reader's interest.

   ....
   ....
   ....
   ....
   ....
   ....

   (2 marks)

   Score: ___ /12

Autumn Term: Workout 5

Warm up

1. Add apostrophes in the correct places in the sentence below.

   This girls book is about peoples everyday lives 700 years ago.

   (1 mark)

Reading Questions

> Mansa Musa was a 14th-century ruler of the prosperous Mali Empire in West Africa, famed for its abundant gold. Sometimes described as history's wealthiest person (a much-disputed claim), he was renowned for flaunting his fortune.
>
> In 1324, Musa set off on a Hajj (a pilgrimage to the sacred Muslim city of Mecca). He was accompanied by around 60 000 men, all wearing the finest Persian silk. En route to Mecca, the party visited Cairo, where Musa lavished the locals with gold from the stores that his elaborate entourage was carrying.

2. Tick the option that is closest in meaning to "prosperous".

   mystical ☐   affluent ☐   vast ☐   influential ☐

   (1 mark)

3. How can you tell that people are unsure if Musa was the richest man in history?

   ....

   ....

   (1 mark)

4. Using a different quote each time, find evidence from the text that suggests Mansa Musa was:

   a) religious.   ....

   b) generous.   ....

   c) extravagant. ....

   (3 marks)

Spelling, Punctuation & Grammar Question

5. Add in the five missing commas to this paragraph.

> Historians know that the people of Mali traded metals like iron copper and gold. Half of the gold in the Old World an area that included Europe Africa and Asia came from just three Malian regions: Bambuk Boure and Galam.

(2 marks)

Writing Question

6. Rewrite this text so that it uses more formal language.

> In 1327, Musa upped sticks and moved his capital to Timbuktu, which he'd conquered earlier. He spent a load of money on improving the city, adding tonnes of new buildings, like a fab palace. Timbuktu was a cool city, where learning, trade and religion were all super important. Things got pretty crazy in 1330 when the city was captured, but Musa retook it quick as a flash.

....

....

....

....

....

....

....

....

(4 marks)

Score: ☐ /12

Autumn Term: Workout 6

Warm up

1. Circle the word which is described in the definition below.

   A word that describes how, where or when something is done.

   adjective   verb   adverb   noun

   (1 mark)

Reading Questions

Deep in the woods lies a palace,
Where the austere King Edwin dwells.
His jester Rollo pesters him,
Then jigs to the jangle of bells.

One day, the King holds a council,
In the walls of the grand citadel.
Rollo makes a joke about taxes,
Then jigs to the jangle of bells.

On hearing Rollo's cutting quip,
The whole room erupts into yells.
Rollo grins with mischievous glee,
Then jigs to the jangle of bells.

"A bit too far?" Rollo wonders,
So to avoid a night in the cells,
He gets up to leave, but first,
He jigs to the jangle of bells.

2. Write down an example of repetition from the poem. What effect does it have?

   ....

   ....
   (2 marks)

3. a) What is the poem's rhyme scheme?

   ....

   b) What effect does this rhyme scheme have?

   ....

   ....
   (2 marks)

Spelling, Punctuation & Grammar Question

4. Rewrite the sentences below so that they use negatives correctly.

   a) The King don't like none of Rollo's jokes.

   ....

   b) Rollo ain't got no chance of getting away with that prank.

   ....
   (2 marks)

Writing Questions

5. The first four lines of a limerick are given below. Write a line to finish the poem. The final line should rhyme with the first two lines.

   > There once was a mischievous clown,
   > Who pocketed the King's golden crown.
   > When the King found out,
   > He let out a shout,

   Limericks have an AABBA rhyme scheme. The first, second and fifth lines are usually 8-10 syllables long.

   ....
   (1 mark)

6. Here are the first two lines of another poem.

   > King Horace had always been mean,
   > But he was no match for his queen.

   Add four more lines to the poem, following this rule:
   Each line must have 8 syllables and be part of a rhyming couplet.

   ....

   ....

   ....

   ....
   (4 marks)

Score: /12

Autumn Term: Workout 7

Warm up

1. What is sensory language?

   ....
   (1 mark)

Reading Questions

> "All aboard!" came the stern call from the platform.
>
> The jostling crowd swept through the train doors like a shoal of fish being drawn into a net. The clamour of animated voices rose briefly to a crescendo before fading into the depths of the train. A sudden silence descended over the platform, heavy with anticipation. Then, as if with relief, the train spurted out a puff of steam, and the brakes unlocked from the iron wheels, which heaved a grateful sigh as they slid over the gunmetal-grey rails.
>
> As the journey wore on, the iron bull settled into a steady canter. It hurtled through valleys, over rivers and between hedgerows, snorting great billows of steam as it went.

2. Find a quote from the text that contains each of these techniques.

   a) Personification ....

   b) Simile ....

   c) Alliteration ....
   (3 marks)

3. Explain the effect of one of the examples you gave in question 2.

   ....

   ....
   (1 mark)

4. The final paragraph is an extended metaphor. What is the effect of this?

   ....

   ....
   (1 mark)

Spelling, Punctuation & Grammar Question

5. Complete these sentences by writing the plural form of the noun in brackets.

   a) Trains hurtled through the countryside like .... *(torpedo)*

   b) Rail services have been affected by a series of .... *(crisis)*

   c) If you look to your left, you will see many rare .... *(fungus)*

   d) Raindrops slashed the train window like .... *(knife)*

   (2 marks)

Writing Questions

6. Rewrite this extract so it is easier to understand.

   Try splitting up the extract into simpler sentences and replacing any unclear words.

   > She shovelled coal into the furnace, and the furnace blazed brightly, and then she shovelled in another, the furnace roared angrily.

   ....

   ....

   ....

   (2 marks)

7. Rewrite this extract so it is more interesting.

   > The train stopped and people got off. It had been a long journey and many of them looked tired. The driver was the last to get off. He didn't look tired at all.

   ....

   ....

   ....

   (2 marks)

   Score: /12

Autumn Term: Workout 8

Warm up

1. Circle the technique used in the phrase "The actor bit off more than he could chew".

   | an oxymoron | irony | an idiom | a simile |

   (1 mark)

Reading Questions

> When I settled in to watch the first episode of *The Splintered Arrow*, I had high hopes. The much-hyped series, which marks legendary director Ryan Raven's first foray into the fantasy genre, appears to have all the ingredients for success. A stellar cast? Tick. A team of experienced writers? Tick. A budget to make your eyes water? Tick. Yet, as the credits rolled, I couldn't help but feel that this particular arrow had fallen wide of the mark. Despite the gorgeous visuals, Raven's world felt stale, populated by lifeless characters churning out formulaic dialogue. As for the story, well, the writers did a botched job of filling in the plot holes. I suppose with only £300 million to spend, the producers had to cut corners somewhere.

2. The writer uses a list of questions to describe the show. What effect does this have?

   ....

   ....
   (1 mark)

3. "I couldn't help but feel that this particular arrow had fallen wide of the mark." What effect does this idiom have?

   ....
   (1 mark)

4. What technique does the writer use in the final sentence? Explain its effect.

   ....

   ....

   ....
   (2 marks)

Spelling, Punctuation & Grammar Question

5. Complete this paragraph by circling the correctly spelt words.

   "I'm not concerned about **unflattering / unflatterring** reviews and idle gossip," Raven said in a recent interview, **refering / referring** to whether or not negative press has affected his desire to continue filming the show. "If anything, I've become more **commited / committed** to the story."

   (3 marks)

Writing Questions

6. Rewrite each sentence to make it more persuasive.

   a) **You should watch this show because it's good.**

   ....

   ....

   b) **I didn't really enjoy watching this TV show.**

   ....

   ....

   (2 marks)

7. Write a short review of a book, film or TV show. Give your opinion and use persuasive language to influence the reader.

   ....

   ....

   ....

   ....

   ....

   (2 marks)

   Score: / 12

Autumn Term: Workout 9

Warm up

1. What does 'characterisation' mean?

   ....
   (1 mark)

Reading Questions

> Shoppers squeeze down busy supermarket aisles. After unloading a trolley laden with goods, a woman named **JOY** approaches the **CASHIER** at one of the tills.
>
> **CASHIER** (scanning goods) Morning! Gosh, the temperature outside's taken a plunge-
>
> **JOY** As has my opinion of this shop. I've been a loyal customer for twenty years, but the service I received here today was abominable. Such a shame.
>
> **CASHIER** (unblinking) I'm so sorry to hear that. May I ask what problem you ha-
>
> **JOY** May you ask? You *should* ask — that's your job, isn't it? Anyway, the fact of the matter is that the speed of today's service was torturous. The staff have no awareness of how their behaviour impacts those around them, they...
>
> As **JOY** continues her tirade, her shopping, scanned by the **CASHIER**, sits unbagged on the counter. Shoppers sigh in the growing queue behind her.

2. a) What impression do you get of Joy?

   ....

   b) Using evidence from the text, explain how the writer makes her seem this way.

   ....

   ....
   (2 marks)

3. How would you describe the cashier's character? Explain your answer.

   ....

   ....
   (2 marks)

Spelling, Punctuation & Grammar Question

4. Circle the correct option to complete each sentence.

   a) Mum called to ask Asif and **me / I** to bring her back a bag of carrots.

   b) My friends and **me / I** weren't sure which aisle would stock marshmallows.

   c) The trolley's squeaky wheels kept making Natalie and **me / I** giggle.

   (3 marks)

Writing Question

5. a) Read the description of Wilbur below. Imagine you're going to write a different play based in a shop, which involves Wilbur and another character. Write a short description of the other character in your play.

   > Wilbur, an eager-to-please shop assistant, loves his job. He's known for being enthusiastic, hard-working and able to think on his feet.

   ....

   ....
   (1 mark)

   b) Now write a few lines from the play in which you demonstrate the character traits of both characters through dialogue and stage directions.

   ....

   ....

   ....

   ....

   ....

   ....
   (3 marks)

   Score: / 12

Autumn Term: Workout 10

Warm up

1. Who might be the intended audience of a leaflet produced by a local politician?

   ....

   (1 mark)

Reading Questions

 A **New Library To Open On Friday**

After much anticipation, Bindley's new library is set to open its doors this week. The library, which was commissioned in the wake of the 2019 Bindley Fire, will provide a haven for book lovers in our town and beyond. We hope you'll join us in celebrating this momentous occasion.

 B **Books Galore, Say No More!**

You'll never believe this — Bindley's brand new library is about to open.
   "I'm so excited," said Paige Turner, a Year 6 pupil at Bindley School. "I love reading and can't wait to see what books there will be."
   There's bound to be an amazing selection. Come on down to see for yourself this Friday!

2. a) Who do you think is the intended audience of Text A?

   ....

   b) Explain how you can tell that the text has been written for this audience.

   ....

   ....

   (2 marks)

3. a) What effect do you think the writer of Text B wants to have on their audience?

   ....

   b) Give an example of a technique the writer uses to achieve this effect. Explain your answer.

   ....

   ....

   (2 marks)

Spelling, Punctuation & Grammar Question

4. For each sentence below, add the missing hyphen in the correct place.

   a) My best friend Manali never leaves the local library empty handed.

   b) I found a dusty crate of thirty five books in the dingy cellar.

   c) The most interesting looking book was always checked out.

   (3 marks)

Writing Question

5. Imagine that you live in Bindley and there is a competition to design a wing of the new library. Plan a letter to the council, in which you explain your ideas for the new wing. Think about how you will structure your letter to make it as convincing as possible.

Introduction	....
	....
1st paragraph	....
	....
2nd paragraph	....
	....
3rd paragraph	....
	....
Conclusion	....
	....

(4 marks)

Score: /12

Autumn Term: Workout 11

Warm up

1. What kind of narrative voice is used in the sentence 'You saw the hill.'? Tick a box.

   first-person ☐   second-person ☐   third-person ☐

   (1 mark)

Reading Questions

> There's nowt but the hint of a breeze,
> To tease the tufts of autumn grass,
> That ring the tarn* below the screes**,
> Where water lies as clear as glass,
> While the flock gathers on the pass.
> It's the dogs tha' do the work, y'know,
> Me, I jus' tell 'em where t' go,
> I whistle to a timeless beat,
> An' watch the dogs weave to an' fro,
> Gatherin' sheep for this year's meet***.
>
> Locked in this dance, this ritual,
> I am one with sheepdogs and sheep,
> These steps have grown habitual,
> 'mongst hills that are in hist'ry steeped,
> An' hist'ry, like the lakes, runs deep.
> I scan the land with westward eyes,
> Beyond the fells where darker skies,
> Hold clouds that gather by the sea,
> An' wonder what those restless tides,
> Might one day bring my sheep an' me.

*tarn — mountain lake   **screes — rocky slopes   ***meet — gathering of sheep farmers

2. Who do you think the narrator is? Give one detail about them.

   ....
   (1 mark)

3. Why do you think the poet uses phonetic spelling?

   ....
   (1 mark)

4. How would you describe the narrator's tone in the final five lines of the poem? Explain your answer using evidence from the text.

   ....

   ....
   (2 marks)

Spelling, Punctuation & Grammar Question

5. Add a comma or commas to each sentence below so that it has the meaning given in brackets underneath.

    a) Two volunteers Rob and Liz will be leading the hike.
    (Two volunteers called Rob and Liz will be leading the hike.)

    b) Amina likes painting the countryside reading maps and fishing.
    (Amina likes painting. She also likes the countryside. She also likes reading maps. She also likes fishing.)

    (2 marks)

Writing Questions

6. Look at the picture on the right.

    a) Write down an interesting adjective to describe:

    the mountains ....

    the kayaker ....

    b) Write down a simile to describe the river.

    ....

    (2 marks)

7. Using your answers to question 6, write four lines of poetry from the perspective of the kayaker in the picture. Describe what you can see and how you feel.

    Your poem doesn't need to rhyme.

    ....

    ....

    ....

    ....

    (3 marks)

Score: /12

Autumn Term: Workout 12

Warm up

1. Which of these is not usually considered part of a novel's context? Tick a box.

   when it was written ☐   where it's set ☐   who the narrator is ☐

   (1 mark)

Reading Questions

> "Edna!" called Mr. Pontellier, her husband, from within, after a few moments had gone by.
> "Don't wait for me," she answered. He thrust his head through the door.
> "You will take cold out there," he said, irritably. "What folly* is this?"
> She heard him moving about the room; every sound indicating impatience and irritation. Another time she would have gone in at his request. She would, through habit, have yielded to his desire; not with any sense of submission or obedience to his compelling wishes, but unthinkingly, as we walk, move, sit, stand, go through the daily treadmill of the life which has been portioned out to us.

*folly — *foolishness*   **An adapted extract from *The Awakening* by Kate Chopin**

2. How does the writer present Mr. Pontellier's attitude towards his wife, Edna? Explain your answer using evidence from the text.

   ....

   ....

   ....

   (2 marks)

3. The extract is from a novel published in 1899. What does the description of Edna suggest about married women's lives at the time? Explain your answer with quotes.

   ....

   ....

   ....

   (2 marks)

Spelling, Punctuation & Grammar Question

4. Write 'A' if the sentence is in the active voice and 'P' if it's in the passive voice.

   a) *The Awakening* was censored for many years after publication. ....

   b) The events of the novel take place in the late 1800s. ....

   c) Chopin's work was only properly appreciated after her death. ....

   (3 marks)

Writing Questions

5. The plot of the first half of *The Awakening* is described below, but it is in the wrong order. Write the numbers 1-4 in the boxes to put the points in the right order.

   Edna falls in love with a man named Robert, who lives at the resort. ☐

   After he leaves, Léonce and Edna return to their home in New Orleans. ☐

   Edna and her husband Léonce are at a holiday resort with their sons. ☐

   Robert leaves for Mexico, realising their relationship can never be. ☐

   (1 mark)

6. Imagine you are Edna and you've just returned from your holiday. Briefly describe your arrival home, then use a flashback to reflect on a moment from your holiday.

   ....

   ....

   ....

   ....

   ....

   (3 marks)

   Score: ☐ /12

Spring Term: Workout 1

Warm up

1. Underline the three prepositions in the sentence below.

   I love sitting by the Seine with a coffee, watching boats drift along the river.

   (1 mark)

Reading Questions

> We are staying in a quaint little maisonette nestled in a leafy Parisian suburb. Adjacent to us is a boulangerie (a bakery), so each morning we are awoken by the smell of freshly baked baguettes — divine!
>
> Paris's alias (the 'City of Love') certainly rings true in the evenings! The streets are full of life and laughter. The illuminated Eiffel Tower becomes a beacon of romance, with countless couples embracing underneath it.
>
> In the daytime, we've kept ourselves busy sauntering around some of the world's most renowned art galleries, not least the Louvre, home to the famous *Mona Lisa* and her much-scrutinised smile. We also squeezed in a visit to the majestic Jardin du Luxembourg. What a beautiful place! I could spend hours strolling amid the flowers and admiring the cityscape in the background.

2. How does the writer feel about Paris? Explain your answer using evidence.

   ....
   ....
   ....
   (2 marks)

3. How does the writer give you a sense of what Paris is like?
   Explain your answer using evidence from the text.

   ....
   ....
   ....
   (2 marks)

Spelling, Punctuation & Grammar Question

4. Give the shortened form of each underlined phrase using an apostrophe.

    a) <u>I would</u> relish the opportunity to visit Paris. ....

    b) <u>They will</u> enjoy the city's exquisite restaurants. ....

    c) It <u>would have</u> been a shame to miss the museum. ....

    (3 marks)

Writing Questions

5. Tick the sentence that is written most effectively to advise tourists visiting Paris.

    The metro is the best way to travel — it's cheap, simple and reliable. ☐

    The Tour Montparnasse is the second ugliest building in the world. ☐

    Don't forget to look before you cross the road. ☐

    (1 mark)

6. Write an article for a travel magazine advising visitors how to spend their time in a place you have visited recently. You should write about:

    | how to get there | what there is to do | where to stay and eat |

    ....

    ....

    ....

    ....

    ....

    ....

    (3 marks)

    Score: ☐ / 12

Spring Term: Workout 2

Warm up

1. If a reader 'infers' something from a text, what are they doing?

   ....

   (1 mark)

Reading Questions

> The lazy hum of the flies, which was ordinarily indistinguishable from the general buzz of animated voices, now filled every corner of the saloon. The waitress, slumped forward at the counter with her angular chin resting in her palms, seemed little more than a piece of furniture. Every so often, she lifted her hand wearily to bat absentmindedly at a fly that flew too close to her face.
>
> At length, the saloon doors swung open and a man walked in. Removing his hat with one hand, he nodded at the waitress and pulled up a seat at the bar. Wordlessly, she reached for a bottle from the cabinet and poured him a drink.

2. Write down an inference you can make from each of the following quotes.

   a) "The lazy hum of the flies [...] filled every corner of the saloon."

   ....

   b) "The waitress [...] seemed little more than a piece of furniture."

   ....

   (2 marks)

3. What can you infer about the relationship between the waitress and the customer? Support your answer with evidence from the text.

   ....

   ....

   ....

   (2 marks)

Spelling, Punctuation & Grammar Question

4. a) Tick the sentence below that uses dashes correctly.

   Clouds of red dust stirred up — by the wind — filled the streets. ☐

   The horserider — a stranger to the town — dismounted warily. ☐

   b) Now rewrite the other sentence so that it uses dashes correctly.

   ....
   (2 marks)

Writing Question

5. a) The text below contains some spelling and grammar mistakes.
   Cross out each mistake and write the correction above it.

   > It had been a long day and the sherif was tired. Arriving back in town, he tied up his horse and enters the jail. He notised at once that something weren't right. The door to the holding cell, which he had left firmly shutted, was now ajar. There was an eery silence. Then, he heard a noise.

   (3 marks)

   b) Now rewrite the text to make it more interesting.

   ....
   ....
   ....
   ....
   ....
   (2 marks)

   Score: ☐ /12

Spring Term: Workout 3

Warm up

1. Complete this sentence, making it as persuasive as possible:

   Vote for me as your leader because ....

   (1 mark)

Reading Questions

> Now, I want to say to you who think women cannot succeed, we have brought the government of England to this position, that it has to face this alternative: either women are to be killed or women are to have the vote. I ask American men in this meeting, what would you say if in your state you were faced with that alternative, that you must either kill them or give them their citizenship? Well, there is only one answer to that alternative, there is only one way out — you must give those women the vote.
>
> So here am I. I come in the intervals of prison appearance. I come after having been four times imprisoned. I come to ask you to help to win this fight.

An abridged extract from a speech by Emmeline Pankhurst in Connecticut, USA in 1913. Pankhurst was a British activist, who campaigned for women to have the right to vote.

2. What is Pankhurst hoping to achieve by giving a speech to this audience?

   ....

   (1 mark)

3. Explain how each of these techniques helps to make her argument more persuasive.

   a) The use of a question to address the audience in the first paragraph

   ....

   ....

   b) The repetition of "I come" in the second paragraph

   ....

   ....

   (2 marks)

Spelling, Punctuation & Grammar Question

4. Circle the correct word to complete each sentence.

   a) Women **which / who** campaigned for the right to vote were called suffragettes.

   b) Emmeline co-founded the Women's Party, **that / which** was set up in 1917.

   c) The man to **who / whom** Emmeline was married was a barrister.

   d) The main goal **who / that** the suffragettes fought for was equal voting rights.

   (4 marks)

Writing Questions

5. a) Imagine you are writing a report about a historical figure who has inspired you. Write the opening sentence of your report, informing the reader about who you have chosen and giving some brief context about their life.

   ....

   ....

   b) Now write a sentence explaining why you find this historical figure inspirational.

   ....

   ....

   (2 marks)

6. Imagine your friend is giving a speech about a historical figure who inspires them. Write a paragraph advising your friend on the language techniques they could use to give a good speech.

   ....

   ....

   ....

   ....

   (2 marks)

Score: ☐ /12

Spring Term: Workout 4

Warm up

1. What is free verse?

   ....

   (1 mark)

Reading Questions

A
A candle on a shelf
Is such a meagre thing,
But if the room is dark,
It makes the darkness sing.
Its radiance is quite paltry;
It cannot banish night,
Yet its glimmer in the shadow
Will always appear bright.

B
The last remnants of the day fade into nothing
As the growing shadows, once proud beings
Of their own, merge like grim phantoms
In the late evening twilight's gathering gloom,
Lost forever in the dusky obscurity.

2. Write 'A' or 'B' next to each statement.

   a) The poem uses figurative language. ......   b) The poem uses juxtaposition. ......

   (1 mark)

3. How does the rhythm of Poem A contrast with the rhythm of Poem B?

   ....

   ....

   (1 mark)

4. Using evidence, compare the tone of Poem A and Poem B.

   ....

   ....

   ....

   (2 marks)

Spelling, Punctuation & Grammar Question

5. Underline the three adjectives in this text. Circle the three adverbs.

> Shadows form when a solid object completely or partially blocks the light. The clearest shadows often form when the light comes from a single point like the Sun or a lamp.

(2 marks)

Writing Question

6. Imagine you have been asked to write a short poem about sunlight.

   a) Write down three descriptive words or phrases you could use in your poem.

   ....

   ....

   (2 marks)

   b) Now write your poem. Include your descriptive words or phrases and:

   | an ABAB rhyme scheme | 8 syllables in each line | a metaphor |

   ....

   ....

   ....

   ....

   ....

   ....

   (3 marks)

   Score: /12

Spring Term: Workout 5

Warm up

1. Rewrite this direct speech so that it is punctuated correctly.

    "It's a murder mystery party", Sam said "and you're invited".

    ....

    (1 mark)

Reading Questions

> Equipped with a cowboy hat, a bandana around his neck and a surprisingly passable Wild Western drawl, Scott had thoroughly got into the swing of his character.
>
> "I'm tellin' ya, Lady Lemoncake is lookin' real snakelike right about now," he mused, pointing in Caitlyn's direction. The other guests turned towards her. Caitlyn, who was nervously examining her nails for the hundredth time that evening, looked up with a start.
>
> "I told you, I'm not interested in killing anyone!" she exclaimed defensively, although the look she shot Scott suggested otherwise. "It can't have been me because..." She looked down at her 'Murder Mystery' playing cards. "...because I was with Anwar. Sorry, I mean 'Captain Codswallop'." She glanced around. "Where is Anwar anyw–"
>
> She was cut short by a bloodcurdling scream from the next room.

2. What is your impression of Caitlyn as a character? Explain your answer.

    ....

    ....

    (2 marks)

3. Do you think the writer intended the story to be more humorous or dramatic? Explain your answer using evidence from the text.

    ....

    ....

    ....

    (2 marks)

Spelling, Punctuation & Grammar Question

4. Add semicolons in the correct places in the sentences below.

   a) The case remains open the detective is pursuing a number of leads.

   b) The gardener and the housekeeper had an alibi the others did not.

   c) Sergeant Spuds has a clear motive Private Peeler's reasons are unclear.

   (3 marks)

Writing Question

5. The essay extracts below are about fictional detectives, but they use quotations badly. Rewrite each extract so the quotations are used effectively. Think about which parts of the quotations are useful and how to fit them into the paragraph.

   A In *A Study in Scarlet*, Sherlock Holmes compares the human mind to an attic. He says, "the skilful workman is very careful indeed as to what he takes into his brain-attic. He will have nothing but the tools which may help him in doing his work, but of these he has a large assortment, and all in the most perfect order." This shows that Holmes is methodical.

   ....

   ....

   ....

   B In *The Murders in the Rue Morgue*, Auguste Dupin, a detective, uses an analogy. Dupin says: He boasted to me, with a low chuckling laugh, that most men, in respect to himself, wore windows in their bosoms. This suggests he knows what people are thinking from their behaviour.

   ....

   ....

   ....

   (4 marks)

Score: /12

Spring Term: Workout 6

> **Warm up**
>
> 1. Circle the best way to end a formal letter to someone whose name you don't know.
>
>   Yours sincerely   Lots of love   Best wishes   Yours faithfully
>
>   *(1 mark)*

Reading Questions

> Dear Ms Sebley,
>
> As Director of Wisham Home Builders, you are doubtless aware that your company recently approved the development of a new housing estate just outside Wisham. On behalf of the local community, I urge you to reverse this decision due to the severe consequences on traffic in the local area and the subsequent risk to the town's cyclists.
>
> I am not a driver, so I frequently cycle around the town. Since moving here in 1998, conditions for cyclists have rapidly deteriorated given the increase of cars on the road. A new estate will attract hundreds of new residents, which will only intensify the issue.
>
> In addition, Wisham simply does not have enough amenities to support the increase in population inevitably brought about by the new housing development.

2. Write down two words to describe the tone of the letter above.
   Find a quote from the text as evidence for each word you have chosen.

   a) **Word 1:** ....

      Evidence: ....

   b) **Word 2:** ....

      Evidence: ....

   (2 marks)

3. What tone might Ms Sebley use to reply? Explain why this tone would be effective.

   ....

   ....

   (2 marks)

Spelling, Punctuation & Grammar Question

4. Underline the subordinating conjunction in each sentence.

   a) Although there are many cyclists in Wisham, the roads have no cycle lanes.

   b) The housing estate will be built unless the council refuses to give permission.

   c) Mara will attend the protest because she wants to protect local cyclists.

(3 marks)

Writing Questions

5. Here is the next part of the letter on page 36, but it has not yet been proofread. Rewrite it, correcting all six spelling and punctuation mistakes.

   > Recent data puts the towns' population at 12 000 and the new estate will provide housing for atleast 600 more. With just a handful of shops restaurants and other facilities, wisham already lacks amenities. Increasing the population without develloping more will worsen the problem grately.

   ....

   ....

   ....

   ....
   (2 marks)

6. Write a new version of the opening paragraph of the letter on page 36, imagining you're in favour of the new housing estate. Use an appropriate tone in your letter.

   ....

   ....

   ....

   ....
   (2 marks)

Score: /12

Spring Term: Workout 7

Warm up

1. What is the purpose of stage directions?

   ....

   (1 mark)

Reading Questions

The curtain lifts on a place that is dark, save for a shaft of light from below which comes up through an open trapdoor in the floor. This slants up and strikes the long leaves and the huge brilliant blossom of a strange plant whose twisted stem projects from right front*. Nothing is seen except this plant and its shadow. A violent wind is heard. A moment later a buzzer. It buzzes once long and three short. Silence. Again the buzzer. Then from below, his shadow blocking the light, comes **ANTHONY**, *a rugged man past middle life; he emerges from the stairway into the room and is seen taking up a phone.*

ANTHONY Yes, Miss Claire? I'll see. *(he brings a thermometer to the stairway for light, looks sharply, then returns to the phone)* It's down to forty-nine. The plants are in danger — *(with great relief and approval)* Oh, that's fine! *(hangs up the receiver)* Fine!

*right front — a location onstage

An adapted extract from *The Verge* by Susan Glaspell

2. Give two ways that the play's staging creates a tense atmosphere.

   ....

   ....

   ....

   (2 marks)

3. How might the actor playing Anthony perform his final word in this extract? What might his tone of voice and body language be like?

   ....

   ....

   (2 marks)

Spelling, Punctuation & Grammar Question

4. Complete the sentences below by circling the correct spelling of the words in bold.

   a) **Nobody / No body** could find **anyway / any way** of saving those flowers.

   b) It **maybe / may be** time to move the plants **into / in to** the greenhouse.

   (2 marks)

Writing Question

5. a) Imagine you are writing a short three-scene play about a man-eating plant. Use the table below to plan your characters and what will happen.

Scene	Characters	What happens
1	....	....
2	....	....
3	....	....

(3 marks)

   b) Now write the opening stage directions for the first scene, describing two different elements of the play's staging.

   ....

   ....

   ....

   (2 marks)

   Score: ☐ /12

Spring Term: Workout 8

Warm up

1. Rewrite this sentence using Standard English: "I'm gonna buy me some suncream."

   ....

   (1 mark)

Reading Questions

> **HOT OFF THE PRESS: BRITAIN BATTLES HORRIFIC HEATWAVE**
>
> Train lines buckling in the heat, shops running out of bottled water, thousands suffering from heat-related illnesses — this is the deeply worrying situation in Britain this week, where temperatures reached an astonishing **38°C**.
>
> Amid extreme temperatures, authorities have warned those vulnerable to the heat to **cover up** or **remain indoors** and to **keep hydrated**. "Make sure you check on vulnerable friends, relatives and neighbours," warned Lucy March, Secretary of State for Health.
>
> 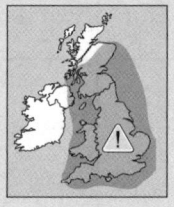 A Red Warning is in force across the majority of the UK, excluding North West Scotland and Northern Ireland.

2. Give two ways that the language used in the headline draws the reader's attention.

   ....

   ....

   (2 marks)

3. Explain how the opening paragraph is effective in encouraging you to keep reading.

   ....

   ....

   (1 mark)

4. Identify one other layout feature used in the text and explain its purpose.

   ....

   ....

   (2 marks)

Spelling, Punctuation & Grammar Question

5. Add commas to each sentence so that they are punctuated correctly.

   a) In the summer I like scuba diving having picnics and playing sports.

   b) Although it was hot Flo who didn't feel the heat was wearing a jumper.

   (2 marks)

Writing Question

6. Imagine you've been asked to answer this essay question:
   'The school summer holidays should be extended by two weeks.
   Do you agree with this statement?'

   a) In note form, write two points you could make to agree with the statement.

   • ....
   • ....
   (1 mark)

   b) In note form, write two points to challenge the statement.

   • ....
   • ....
   (1 mark)

   c) Write a short paragraph for one of your points from part a) or part b).
      Include some evidence to support your point.

   ....
   ....
   ....
   ....
   (2 marks)

Score: /12

Spring Term: Workout 9

Warm up

1. What is enjambment?

   ....

   (1 mark)

Reading Questions

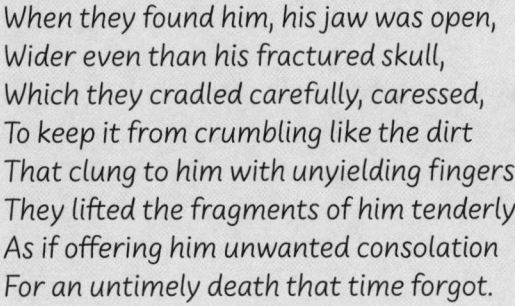

When they found him, his jaw was open,
Wider even than his fractured skull,
Which they cradled carefully, caressed,
To keep it from crumbling like the dirt
That clung to him with unyielding fingers.
They lifted the fragments of him tenderly,
As if offering him unwanted consolation
For an untimely death that time forgot.

Impossible for him to comprehend,
Modern-day men pick at his broken body,
Ripping through the fabric of a millennium,
Even with their brushes' soft sweep.
Perhaps they felt him by their side,
The spirit of a man led by different rulers,
Spoken of in some long-forgotten tongue,
Who once lived under the very same stars.

2. "Which they cradled carefully, caressed, / To keep it from crumbling"
   What is the effect of the alliteration in these lines?

   ....

   (1 mark)

3. "the dirt / That clung to him with unyielding fingers"
   Which technique is used here, and what does this technique suggest?

   ....

   ....

   (2 marks)

4. 'The poem implies that unearthing an ancient skeleton is wrong.'
   Copy a metaphor that supports this statement and explain its effect.

   ....

   ....

   ....

   (2 marks)

Spelling, Punctuation & Grammar Question

5. Read the passage below, which hasn't been split into paragraphs.
   Add two paragraph markers (//) to divide it into three paragraphs.

   > In the late 8th century AD, the Vikings carried out their first raid on Britain. Arriving on fast-moving longships, they attacked the monastery of Lindisfarne in Northumberland, stealing various items and killing many monks.   The first raid of many, it marked the start of Viking settlement in Britain.   For many decades, the Viking capital of England was York, then known as Jorvik.   The Vikings may have chosen this location because of its strategic advantages.   York was accessible from the coast and it was situated between two rivers, making it easy to defend.   In the 1970s, archaeologists discovered the remains of various Viking artefacts in an area of York called Coppergate.   Extensive excavations revealed thousands of artefacts, from clothing and pottery to building materials and animal bones.   These have allowed us to learn much more about how the Vikings lived.

   (2 marks)

Writing Question

6. Imagine you are an archaeologist who has just discovered
   a strange artefact buried underground.

   a) Briefly describe the artefact. Use interesting or unusual adjectives.

   ....
   (1 mark)

   b) Now write down a simile to describe either the artefact or a part of it.

   ....
   (1 mark)

   c) Write four lines of poetry about the moment the artefact was discovered.
      Use your answers to parts a) and b) to help you.

   ....

   ....

   ....

   ....
   (2 marks)

   Score: /12

Spring Term: Workout 10

Warm up

1. Underline the words in the sentence below that create a mysterious atmosphere.

   The creaking sign was swiftly hidden by the foggy night air.

   (1 mark)

Reading Questions

> In the corners hung spiders' webs; in the rooms stood dust in heaps; pigeons built their nests in the cornices* and sparrows in the beams. Heaps of withered leaves lay rotting in the garden; weeds grew over the tanks; the flower-beds were hidden by jungle. There were jackals in the court-yard, and rats in the granary**; mould and fungus were everywhere to be seen; musk-rats and centipedes swarmed in the rooms; bats flew about night and day. The cornice of the house was broken in places, as were the sashes***, the shutters, and the railings. The matting was soaked with rain; there was dust on the painted walls. Over the bookcases were the dwellings of insects; straws from the sparrows' nests on the glass of the chandeliers. In the house there was no mistress, and without a mistress paradise itself would be a ruin.

*cornices — *ledges*   **granary — *grain store*
***sashes — *parts of a window*

An abridged extract from *The Poison Tree* by Bankim Chandra Chatterjee

2. a) Circle the adjective that best describes the setting.

   | breathtaking | ramshackle | isolated | deceptive |

   b) Explain your answer to part a) using evidence from the text.

   ....

   ....
   (2 marks)

3. The sentences in the first half of the extract are structured in a similar way. What is this similarity and what effect does it have on the reader?

   ....

   ....
   (2 marks)

Spelling, Punctuation & Grammar Question

4. Circle the correct spelling of the words in bold.

    a) The building's **colums / columns** are **beggining / beginning** to crumble.

    b) The **campaigner / campainer** saved the **extraordinary / extrordinary** building.

    (2 marks)

Writing Questions

5. Rewrite the text below so the description of the setting creates a hectic atmosphere.

    > Vast screens, like empty canvases, still hung above the cobwebbed airport check-in desks. But no one had checked in recently, let alone boarded a flight.

    ....

    ....

    (2 marks)

6. Write a paragraph describing one of the settings below.
   Use interesting vocabulary and sentence structures to create a certain atmosphere.

    | an abandoned factory | a ruined manor | a collapsed bridge |

    ....

    ....

    ....

    ....

    ....

    (3 marks)

Score: /12

Spring Term: Workout 11

> **Warm up**
>
> 1. Underline the examples of onomatopoeia in this sentence.
>
>   **Waves crashed against the boat whilst rain pattered down onto the deck.**
>
>   *(1 mark)*

Reading Questions

> LOCAL WOMAN SAILS AROUND BRITAIN IN BATHTUB
>
> Tapton's Amy Soams made history this week as she completed her sea voyage around the British Isles. It's a fantastic feat, and one made all the more impressive by the fact that Soams carried out the venture in a small bathtub from her local DIY store. When she begins talking, her passions for bathroom fittings and sailing are immediately obvious.
>
> "The hardest part," she recalls, "was choosing a suitable bath. Baths are like waves — there are so many of them, but each one is unique!"

2. Which technique is used in "fantastic feat"? Explain its effect.

   ....

   ....
   (2 marks)

3. What is the effect of the simile "Baths are like waves"?

   ....

   ....
   (1 mark)

4. Why do you think the writer uses the present tense in the extract?

   ....

   ....
   (1 mark)

Spelling, Punctuation & Grammar Question

5. Fill in the gap in each sentence using either 'who's' or 'whose'.

   a) .... the woman who sailed around Britain in a bathtub?

   b) Amy, ... voyage was followed by many news channels, is famous.

   c) Is there anyone .... ever attempted a journey like this before?

   (3 marks)

Writing Questions

6. Rewrite this sentence so that it uses two different persuasive techniques.

   If you're looking for a new hobby, you should try sailing.

   ....

   ....
   (2 marks)

7. For her next adventure, Amy will attempt to cross the Atlantic in a hot tub. Write a paragraph persuading people to sponsor her trip. You may wish to use some of the following arguments.

   | It is important to support women's sports. | It will encourage young people to be more active. | Amy is a source of local and national pride. |

   ....

   ....

   ....

   ....

   ....
   (2 marks)

Score: /12

Spring Term: Workout 12

Warm up

1. What is the difference in meaning between 'its' and 'it's'?

   ....

   (1 mark)

Reading Questions

> The hot air balloon rose up, slowly and serenely. The men and women in the crowd below watched, rapt with awe, like children fascinated by a new toy. Étienne Montgolfier smiled to himself. This was his moment, the moment all of France had come to see: humanity defying the very laws of nature, rising above the constraints of such trivialities as gravity. Many had accused him of recklessness, but Étienne preferred to see himself as a pioneer, an explorer venturing into uncharted territory — and how could one be a pioneer if one never took risks? In any case, this flight, staged at the Palace of Versailles in the royal presence, carried only a sheep, a duck and a rooster. It would have been unwise to send a human at this stage; after all, no one knew if humans could survive, separated from the Earth's grounding influence. Human flight would surely come, in time.

2. In this fictional account of a real event, the writer uses a simile.
   Copy the simile, then explain what impression it gives you.

   ....

   ....
   (2 marks)

3. Why do you think the writer uses alliteration in the phrase "slowly and serenely"?

   ....

   ....
   (1 mark)

4. What effect does the writer's use of a rhetorical question have on the reader?

   ....

   ....
   (1 mark)

Spelling, Punctuation & Grammar Question

5. Rewrite the sentences below using the past perfect form.

   a) I take off. ....

   b) They fly. ....

   (2 marks)

Writing Questions

6. Write a sentence to describe each of the following, using the language technique given in brackets.

   a) a crowd (hyperbole)

   ....

   b) the wind (onomatopoeia)

   ....

   (2 marks)

7. Imagine you are a passenger on a hot air balloon. Using three language techniques, write a short paragraph describing your experience.

   ....

   ....

   ....

   ....

   ....

   (3 marks)

Score: /12

Summer Term: Workout 1

Warm up

1. Rewrite the following sentence, correcting any spelling mistakes.

   The new dish past the taste test — it had a positive affect on diners.

   ....

   (1 mark)

Reading Questions

A Last week, I had the pleasure of eating at 'The Flying Pufferfish' in Top Middleton. And what a meal it was! The soup of the day was excellent, and the rainbow trout was to die for. Dessert was also sublime — my chocolate fondant melted in the mouth. It's not the cheapest place in town, but it's without a doubt the best!

B 'The Flying Pufferfish' on Port Street specialises in fish dishes and puddings. Though expensive by the town's standards, it has generally received positive reviews and remains popular with locals and tourists alike.

No bookings. Children's menu available. Limited vegetarian options.

2. Describe the tone of Text A. Explain your answer using evidence from the text.

   ....

   ....

   ....

   (2 marks)

3. How does the tone of Text B differ from the tone of Text A? Why do you think this is the case?

   ....

   ....

   (2 marks)

Spelling, Punctuation & Grammar Question

4. Complete each sentence by circling the correct words in bold.

   Sue wants to **borrow / lend** a cookbook from me (the one I **borrowed / lent** you).

   She tried to **teach / learn** me a new recipe but I had already **taught / learnt** it.

   (2 marks)

Writing Questions

5. Proofread this extract from The Flying Pufferfish's website.
   Underline each mistake and write the correction above it.

   Are you celebrating a special occassion? Why not celebrate it with us. We offer private rooms for up to 70 guests and a bespoke menu and a complementary decorating service. contact are knowledgable team today.

   (3 marks)

6. Rewrite the text below, making it clearer by splitting it into shorter sentences and using appropriate conjunctions.

   'The Flying Pufferfish' in Top Middleton was recently inspected by the council's food standards team who found that urgent improvement is required, recommending a temporary closure of the venue which means that customers should make alternative dining arrangements — this issue will be resolved by the end of January.

   ....

   ....

   ....

   ....

   ....

   ....

   (2 marks)

   Score: /12

Summer Term: Workout 2

Warm up

1. Fill in the gaps by writing the simple past tense form of each verb in brackets.

   We .... *(to go)* to swim, but the waves .... *(to be)* too rough.

   (1 mark)

Reading Questions

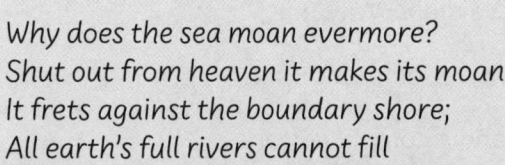

> Why does the sea moan evermore?
> Shut out from heaven it makes its moan.
> It frets against the boundary shore;
> All earth's full rivers cannot fill
> The sea, that drinking thirsteth still.
>
> Sheer miracles of loveliness
> Lie hid in its unlooked-on bed:
> Anemones, salt, passionless,
> Blow flower-like; just enough alive
> To blow and multiply and thrive.

An extract from 'By the Sea' by Christina Rossetti

2. Find an example of personification in the first stanza.
   What does this suggest about the sea?

   ....

   ....
   (1 mark)

3. Why do you think the writer uses enjambment towards the end of the first stanza?

   ....

   ....
   (1 mark)

4. How is the sea presented differently in the second stanza compared to the first?
   Explain your answer using evidence from the text.

   ....

   ....

   ....
   (2 marks)

Spelling, Punctuation & Grammar Question

5. Underline the word in each phrase that should have an apostrophe. Then write the correct spelling of the word on the line.

   a) the two famous marine <u>biologists</u> boats ....

   b) an excess of <u>childrens</u> life jackets ....

   (2 marks)

Writing Question

6. a) Rewrite this paragraph so that it is grammatically correct and makes sense.

   Located in the Pacific Ocean, the Mariana Trench are the most deep point of the world's oceans. At an almost depth of 11 km, it is real devoid of light.

   ....

   ....

   ....
   (2 marks)

   b) Write a few lines of poetry about the bottom of the Mariana Trench. In your poem, you should use:

   | the present tense | two interesting adverbs | a passive verb |

   ....

   ....

   ....

   ....

   ....
   (3 marks)

   Score: /12

Summer Term: Workout 3

Warm up

1. What is meant by juxtaposition?

   ....

   (1 mark)

Reading Questions

> Madame Defarge, his wife, sat in the shop behind the counter as he came in. Madame Defarge was a stout woman, with a watchful eye that seldom seemed to look at anything, a large hand heavily ringed, a steady face, strong features, and great composure of manner. There was a character about Madame Defarge, from which one might have predicated* that she did not often make mistakes against herself in any of the reckonings** over which she presided. Her knitting was before her, but she had laid it down to pick her teeth with a toothpick. Thus engaged, with her right elbow supported by her left hand, Madame Defarge said nothing, but coughed just one grain of cough. This, in combination with the lifting of her darkly defined eyebrows by the breadth of a line, suggested to her husband that he would do well to look round the shop among the customers.

*predicated — *stated*
**reckonings — *opinions*

An abridged extract from *A Tale of Two Cities* by Charles Dickens

2. a) Find and copy an example of juxtaposition used to describe Madame Defarge.

   ....

   b) What does this example suggest about her?

   ....

   (2 marks)

3. Write down an adjective that sums up Madame Defarge's character.
   Explain your choice of adjective using evidence from the text.

   ....

   ....

   ....

   (2 marks)

Spelling, Punctuation & Grammar Question

4. Underline the subordinate clauses in these complex sentences.

   a) Until Dickens was four years old, he lived in the city of Portsmouth.

   b) Dickens advocated for the poor because they were often mistreated by the rich.

   c) He was buried in Westminster Abbey despite his request to be buried in Kent.

   (3 marks)

Writing Questions

5. Rewrite the paragraph so that it uses the quotation correctly.

   > Madame Defarge's husband is presented as an intimidating character. "a bull-necked, martial-looking man." This language related to strength and aggression suggests he would not be easily beaten in a fight.

   ....

   ....

   ....

   (1 mark)

6. Here is a description of a nobleman from another part of *A Tale of Two Cities*.

   > He was a man of about sixty, handsomely dressed, haughty in manner, and with a face like a fine mask. A face of a transparent paleness; every feature in it clearly defined; one set expression on it.

   Write a paragraph explaining how Dickens presents the nobleman. Include three separate quotations in your answer and embed them correctly.

   ....

   ....

   ....

   ....

   ....

   (3 marks)

Score: /12

Summer Term: Workout 4

> **Warm up**
>
> 1. Which technique is used in the following sentence?
>
>   It's colder than the Arctic in my friend's house.   ....
>
>   *(1 mark)*

Reading Questions

> In 1972, I was tasked with retrieving some documents from an enemy base deep in the frozen north, a land home only to howling wolves and a small number of unfortunate residents who would give anything to be elsewhere. I arrived in the vicinity early and spent the next two days acclimatising, which in practice meant alternately pacing up and down and trying to sleep in my perishingly cold tent. The wind was my constant — and only — companion, and I felt it deeply. Temperatures plummeted when night fell, but my palms still felt sweaty as I cut the wire fence surrounding the site.

2. The text says that the writer spent two days "acclimatising".
   What does this suggest about the conditions in the area?

   ....

   ....
                                                                                    (1 mark)

3. "The wind was my constant — and only — companion, and I felt it deeply."
   What does the following quote suggest about how the narrator is feeling?

   ....
                                                                                    (1 mark)

4. How does the writer feel as he begins his mission? How do you know?

   ....

   ....

   ....
                                                                                    (2 marks)

Spelling, Punctuation & Grammar Question

5. Write 'c' or 's' in the gaps in these sentences so that the words are spelt correctly.

   I often asked my grandma for advi__e.   I had to practi__e every single day.

   In 1969, I received my pilot's licen__e.   We devi__ed a shelter against the storm.

   The agency performs a vital servi__e.   The spy convin__ed the other officer.

   (3 marks)

Writing Question

6. Imagine you have been asked to write an essay that has the following title: 'It is better to live in a place that experiences a variety of temperatures than a place where it is mild all year round.' How far do you agree?

   a) Write down four points you could make in your essay.

   - ....
   - ....
   - ....
   - ....

   (2 marks)

   b) Write a paragraph about one of your points from part a).
      Make sure you fully explain your point and provide evidence to support it.

   ....

   ....

   ....

   ....

   (2 marks)

   Score: ☐ /12

Summer Term: Workout 5

Warm up

1. What is a protagonist?

   ....

   (1 mark)

Reading Questions

A I crane my neck and peer into the sky in an attempt to locate the top of the imposing concrete building that symbolises all that is wrong with my city. Finding my efforts in vain, I transfer my attention to the entrance, a great, gaping mouth swallowing up a constant flow of faceless men and women, most glued to their holochips. It is one of these drab, servile workers that I must find. And soon.

B The city was not at all as Mia had expected. It did not look like it was on the brink of collapse: the streets were tidy and the people appeared prosperous. Mia stared out of the window of the hoverbus, suddenly unsure. Looks can be deceiving, she thought. Still, this was not the place she'd imagined.

2. Tick the boxes to show whether each sentence refers to Text A, Text B or both.

	A	B
a) The text uses third-person narration.	☐	☐
b) The text uses a metaphor.	☐	☐
c) The protagonist came to the city with an aim.	☐	☐

   (3 marks)

3. Compare how the protagonists of Text A and Text B feel about their situation. Support your answer using evidence from each text.

   ....

   ....

   ....

   (2 marks)

Spelling, Punctuation & Grammar Question

4. Rewrite these sentences so that they include a colon.

   a) We had two options stay and struggle or leave the city.

   ....

   b) There is one single mode of transport a hoverbus.

   ....

   (2 marks)

Writing Questions

5. Read this story summary, then write the opening paragraph of the story so that it grabs the reader's attention.

   > The government replaces all the teachers at Kate's school with boring, strict robots. The students plot to destroy the robots.

   ....

   ....

   ....

   ....

   (2 marks)

6. Write the opening paragraph of another story. Your paragraph should create a sense of mystery, and include the following:

   | a secretive character | an urban setting | futuristic technology |

   ....

   ....

   ....

   ....

   (2 marks)

Score: ☐ /12

Summer Term: Workout 6

Warm up

1. Circle the misspelt word in this sentence. Then, write the correction on the line.

   Squirrels are my favourite animal — their so fun to watch. ....
   (1 mark)

Reading Questions

> **SOS: SAVE OUR SQUIRRELS**
>
> Red squirrels are smaller and much less common than their grey counterparts. Unfortunately, they are at serious risk of extinction, in part due to a disease called squirrelpox, which is carried by grey squirrels. This disease is highly transmissible and can quickly kill populations of red squirrels whilst generally leaving greys untouched.
>
> Help us ensure that red squirrels remain a part of Britain's wildlife for generations to come.
>
> **How can I help?**
> - Join your local red squirrel network
> - Report any red squirrel sightings
> - Keep your pets away from reds

2. a) Who is the writer's intended audience? How do you know?

   ....

   ....
   (1 mark)

   b) What tone does the writer use? Why is this tone effective for this audience?

   ....

   ....
   (2 marks)

3. How has the writer used language to emphasise the severity of the threat that red squirrels face? Use one piece of evidence from the text in your answer.

   ....

   ....
   (2 marks)

Spelling, Punctuation & Grammar Question

4. Add a hyphen in the correct place in each sentence.

   a) Kielder Forest is a squirrel friendly zone in northern England.

   b) Red squirrels are beautiful looking animals that must be protected.

   c) Both red and grey squirrels eat lots of seeds and sweet tasting berries.

   (3 marks)

Writing Question

5. a) Here are some points from an article entitled 'How can we care for urban wildlife?' Number the sentences 1-4 to put them in the correct order.

   Strategies must be put in place to protect these animals' habitats. ☐

   We don't often think about wildlife within cities. ☐

   However, birds, waterfowl and even some larger mammals live in cities. ☐

   Furthermore, gardeners should leave some wild areas for insects. ☐

   (1 mark)

   b) Write a conclusion for the article. Think carefully about how you will structure your conclusion so that it reads logically and sums up the article.

   ....

   ....

   ....

   ....

   ....

   (2 marks)

Score: ☐ /12

Summer Term: Workout 7

Warm up

1. What is a stanza?

   ....

   (1 mark)

Reading Questions

> An idle lingerer on the wayside's road,
> He gathers up his work and yawns away;
> A little longer, ere* the tiresome load
> Shall be reduced to ashes or to clay.
>
> His mission? Well, there is but one,
> And if it is a mission he knows it, nay,
> To be a happy idler, to lounge and sun,
> And dreaming, pass his long-drawn days away.
>
> So dreams he on, his happy life to pass
> Content, without ambition's painful sighs,
> Until the sands run down into the glass;
> He smiles—content—unmoved and dies.
>
> And yet, with all the pity that you feel
> For this poor mothling of that flame, the world;
> Are you the better for your desperate deal,
> When you, like him, into eternity are hurled?

*ere — before

An adapted extract from 'The Idler' by Alice Moore Dunbar-Nelson

2. Circle the box that contains a theme found in the poem above.

   | conflict | celebration | time | family |

   (1 mark)

3. Is laziness presented positively or negatively in the poem?
   Use evidence from the text to explain your answer.

   ....

   ....

   (2 marks)

4. How does the writer present the theme of ambition?
   Explain your answer using evidence from the text.

   ....

   ....

   (2 marks)

Spelling, Punctuation & Grammar Question

5. Fill in the gaps using 'ei' or 'ie' so that each word is spelt correctly.

   a) My n....ghbour ach....ved his life's ambition.

   b) My fr....nd's goal is to live in a for....gn country.

   (2 marks)

Writing Question

6. Imagine you are writing a poem about a journey on foot down a long road.

   a) Write an interesting simile describing what you can see.

   ....
   (1 mark)

   b) The first line of the poem is given below. Finish the remaining lines of the poem, describing what you can see, hear, smell, taste and touch on your journey. In your poem, you should include an example of:

   | sensory language | onomatopoeia | alliteration |

   I travel on, through changing scenes and changing moods,

   I can see ....

   I can hear ....

   I can smell ....

   I can taste ....

   I can touch ....
   (3 marks)

Score: ..... /12

Summer Term: Workout 8

Warm up

1. Rewrite this sentence, adding punctuation marks in the correct places.

   It's not possible she exclaimed

   ....

   (1 mark)

Reading Questions

> Chaos. That was the only way he could describe it. He'd gone to work as normal, although no one else had bothered, and really, who could blame them? Most things relevant to his job had ceased to function: his computer programmes weren't loading, his emails were inaccessible, and any relevant data stored online was unreachable.
>
> Similar scenes of chaos had played out across the country. The banking system was in tatters. Trains had stopped in their tracks. Planes were grounded, shops shuttered, schools in disorder. The prime minister had been moved to a secure location at the first sign of trouble, where she now sat wondering what to do. Conspiracy theorists had long imagined such a scenario, but everyone knew it would never actually happen.
>
> Until, this morning, it had.
>
> 06:36 am, 23rd April. St George's Day. The day the internet disappeared.

2. How does the writer grab the reader's attention at the start of the text?

   ....

   (1 mark)

3. The text shifts in focus in the second paragraph. What effect does this have?

   ....

   ....

   (1 mark)

4. What effect is created by the structure of the final three sentences?

   ....

   ....

   (1 mark)

Spelling, Punctuation & Grammar Question

5. Add a pair of brackets to each of the sentences below.

   a) My computer which is now very old runs incredibly slowly .

   b) Robots both big and small ones will be everywhere in the future .

   c) I need the internet to complete a task at school a history essay .

   (3 marks)

Writing Question

6. Imagine you've been asked to write a short story about a new technological invention that goes wrong.

   a) Write a short description of the new invention.

   ....
   (1 mark)

   b) Briefly describe what goes wrong with this invention.

   ....
   (1 mark)

   c) Write the opening paragraph of your story, structuring your paragraph to create suspense. Use interesting vocabulary and a range of language techniques.

   ....

   ....

   ....

   ....

   ....

   ....
   (3 marks)

Score: /12

Summer Term: Workout 9

Warm up

1. Why might a writer use descriptive language in a travel guide?

   ....
   (1 mark)

Reading Questions

> Naqsh-e Jahan Square, built by the Persian ruler Abbas the Great in the early 1600s, is the most famous landmark in the Iranian city of Isfahan. This large oblong of verdant grass and paved walkways is surrounded by a stunning architectural ensemble of royal palaces and ornate mosques. A place of soaring minarets, towering domes and lofty arches, the square is a spot where the cries of locals, visitors and shopkeepers mingle with the splashing of fountains, and the aroma of freshly brewed coffee fills the air. On the southern and eastern sides stand two mosques, both hushed havens of peace in the middle of a clamorous city. With their vivid mosaics, these mosques are masterpieces of Iranian-Islamic architecture.

2. The square is "A place of soaring minarets, towering domes and lofty arches". What effect does this phrase have on the reader and how is that effect created?

   ....

   ....
   (2 marks)

3. How does the writer create a calming tone when describing the mosques?

   ....

   ....
   (1 mark)

4. What do you think the writer's purpose is?
   Explain your answer using evidence from the text.

   ....

   ....
   (2 marks)

Spelling, Punctuation & Grammar Question

5. Rewrite the first sentence using the active voice and the second sentence using the passive voice.

   a) Isfahan was named the capital city by Abbas the Great.

   ....

   b) Today, almost 2 million people inhabit the city.

   ....
   (2 marks)

Writing Questions

6. This text contains spelling, punctuation and grammar mistakes. Circle each mistake and write the correction above it.

   > Isfahan, that is Irans third largest city, has a historic and senic bridge across its main river. However the river underneath the bridge often runs dry.

   (2 marks)

7. Rewrite this text so that it flows better and doesn't repeat itself.

   > Chaharbagh (meaning 'four gardens') is a long tree-lined avenue in central Isfahan. It was built in 1596. It is famous because it is beautiful. Many tourists visit it. Locals also visit it. It is a popular place for socialising.

   ....

   ....

   ....

   ....

   ....
   (2 marks)

Score: /12

Summer Term: Workout 10

Warm up

1. Which of these are part of a play's staging? Circle all that apply.

   | the props | the lighting | the dialogue | the set | the themes |

   (1 mark)

Reading Questions

*A feast is taking place in a castle. Various **NOBLEMEN** are sat around a table with **KING ARTHUR** at the head. The scene is lit by candles. All of a sudden, the candles go out. Cries of panic are heard. Enter a **KNIGHT**, seen by moonlight. Silence.*
ARTHUR: Who is this who dares enter my hall? Name yourself, stranger.
KNIGHT: My name is mine alone. But know this, Arthur, King of Britain. I am that which you most fear and that which you most need, the sword at your neck and the air you breathe. Now, who will answer my summons?
ARTHUR: Wha— What right have you to issue such a challenge?
KNIGHT: Like the peasant outside the gate, I claim no right. Nonetheless, this is my summons: meet me in the Greenwood on this day a year hence.
*Exit **KNIGHT**. The candles re-ignite, seemingly of their own accord.*

2. a) Circle the box that best describes the atmosphere in this scene.

   | mysterious | carefree | mournful | peaceful |

   b) Explain your answer to part a).

   ....

   ....
   (2 marks)

3. How does the writer present the knight?
   Explain your answer using evidence from the text.

   ....

   ....

   ....
   (2 marks)

Spelling, Punctuation & Grammar Question

4. Underline the incorrectly spelt word in each sentence. Write the correct spelling on the line.

   a) The strange old wizard spoke sternly to the monach. ....

   b) The mischevous sprites caused havoc on the journey. ....

   c) The scolar had spent her life studying magic swords. ....

   (3 marks)

Writing Question

5. Write a short opening scene for a play based on the summary below. Think carefully about the atmosphere you want to create. Include stage directions and format the dialogue correctly.

   > It's 2022. Nicola is hiking in Scotland. She meets a man dressed in armour who claims he's an ancient king destined to win a great battle. Nicola is sceptical — and intrigued.

   ....

   ....

   ....

   ....

   ....

   ....

   ....

   ....

   ....

   (4 marks)

   Score: /12

Summer Term: Workout 11

Warm up

1. Give one reason why it is useful to include subheadings in a report.

   ....
   (1 mark)

Reading Questions

> A Report on the Risk of Injury among Swimmers in Piranha-infested Waters
>
> **1.** Our research indicates that there is a strong link between swimming with piranhas and being admitted to A&E. People who regularly swim in piranha-infested waters are 51% more likely to need emergency medical treatment than the UK average (see graph).
> **2.** Of those who regularly swim with piranhas, the group with the highest level of hospital admittance was those with the fewest qualifications; only 3.2% of those holding a Level 5 Piranha Swimming Safety Certificate attend A&E each year, compared to 85% of piranha swimmers without any formal qualifications.
> **3.** Most victims only suffered slight damage to their toes and fingers and were able to return home the same day. Around 15% of victims had more serious injuries and spent over 48 hours recovering in hospital.
> **4.** Given the above information, we strongly recommend against swimming with piranhas.

2. Why might the writer have chosen to include a diagram? Explain your answer.

   ....

   ....

   ....
   (2 marks)

3. Do you think the structure of the text as a whole is effective?
   Is there anything you would change? Explain your answer.

   ....

   ....

   ....
   (2 marks)

Spelling, Punctuation & Grammar Question

4. Add commas so that each sentence is punctuated correctly.

   a) Piranhas a type of fish from South America are classed as omnivores.

   b) Although they are famous for their sharp teeth serious attacks are rare.

   (2 marks)

Writing Question

5. Imagine you are writing an essay entitled 'It is cruel to keep fish as pets. Discuss.'

   a) Write down four points you could make in your essay.

   - ....
   - ....
   - ....
   - ....

   (2 marks)

   b) Choose your strongest point and write a paragraph for it. Make sure you fully explain your point and provide evidence to support it. You should refer to an opposing point of view and explain why you disagree with it.

   ....
   ....
   ....
   ....
   ....
   ....
   ....

   (3 marks)

   Score: /12

Summer Term: Workout 12

Warm up

1. Which of these pairs of words are half rhymes? Tick a box.

   golden / goal ☐   wait / plate ☐   ridge / badge ☐

   (1 mark)

Reading Questions

A

Soldier, rest! thy warfare o'er,
Sleep the sleep that knows not breaking;
Dream of battled fields no more,
Days of danger, nights of waking.
In our isle's enchanted hall,
Hands unseen thy couch are strewing*,
Fairy strains of music fall,
Every sense in slumber dewing**.

An extract from 'Soldier Rest' by Sir Walter Scott

B

Move him into the sun—
Gently its touch awoke him once,
At home, whispering of fields half-sown.
Always it woke him, even in France,
Until this morning and this snow.
If anything might rouse him now
The kind old sun will know.

An extract from 'Futility' by Wilfred Owen

*strewing — *spreading*   **dewing — *dampening*

2. The poems above use a similar metaphor to describe the death of a soldier in battle. Explain what this metaphor is, supporting your answer with a quote from one poem.

   ....

   ....

   ....

   (2 marks)

3. a) Briefly explain how the poems use rhyme differently.

   ....

   b) What is the effect of this rhyme scheme in Text B?

   ....

   ....

   (2 marks)

Spelling, Punctuation & Grammar Question

4. Fill in each gap with either 'c' or 't' so that the words are spelt correctly.

   a) As the battle began, both armies were soaked by torren___ial rain.

   b) Although war has a finan___ial cost, the biggest impact is the loss of life.

   c) The term 'mar___ial arts' covers a wide range of combat techniques.

   (3 marks)

Writing Question

5. Here are the opening lines to a different poem by Wilfred Owen called 'Dulce et Decorum Est'. In these lines, Owen uses similes to describe soldiers marching.

   > Bent double, like old beggars under sacks,
   > Knock-kneed, coughing like hags, we cursed through sludge,

   a) Here's another poem about war. Fill in the gaps with appropriate similes.

   > Bombs fell around us like ....
   >
   > While gunfire overhead tore holes in night's thick cloak,
   >
   > Like ...., we crept forward,
   >
   > Groping through the mud and reeling through the smoke.

   (2 marks)

   b) Now add two lines to the poem in part a), using at least one poetic technique. Make sure your second line rhymes with 'cloak' and 'smoke'.

   ....

   ....

   (2 marks)

Score: /12

Answers

Autumn Term

Workout 1 — pages 2-3

1. We <u>brought</u> back some sweets that we <u>bought</u> on holiday. *(1 mark)*
2. a) E.g. a speech
   b) E.g. an advert
   c) E.g. a story
   (1 mark for all correct)
3. a) E.g. rhetorical question, imperatives, rule of three
   b) E.g. Both writers are trying to persuade the reader to do something.
   (1 mark for each)
4. E.g. It makes the peacefulness and silence of the scene stand out even more. *(1 mark)*
5. a) Our <u>gracious</u> hosts at the chalet offered us a <u>nutritious</u> breakfast.
   b) Tackling that slope is <u>ambitious</u> — my last attempt was <u>atrocious</u>.
   (1 mark for each sentence)
6. Any sensible answers.
   (1 mark for each row of the table)

Workout 2 — pages 4-5

1. You could have underlined e.g. figurative language, describe, city's appearance
   (1 mark for underlining at least two of the words or phrases above)
2. a) E.g. They thought it was run-down and miserable.
   b) E.g. They thought it was pretty.
   (1 mark for each)
3. E.g. The hyperbole of "you can buy everything under the sun" in Text A makes modern-day Drabston seem great. However, in Text B, using the rule of three ("beauty, charm and tranquillity") suggests Drabston was nicer in the past.
   (1 mark for explaining a technique in Text A, 1 mark for explaining a technique in Text B)
4. Drabston was supposed to be a <u>temporary</u> home, but after visiting one <u>Wednesday</u>, my dad decided to move here <u>permanently</u> and <u>signed</u> a contract to buy a house.
   (1 mark for every 2 words underlined and corrected)
5. a) Any sensible answers.
   (1 mark for each detailed main point that addresses the prompt)
   b) Any sensible answer.
   (1 mark for addressing the prompt, 1 mark for outlining your argument)

Workout 3 — pages 6-7

1. E.g. An idea or feeling that a word brings to mind. *(1 mark)*
2. E.g. She cares about them a lot, since "She'd tend to them for hours".
   (1 mark for describing her attitude, 1 mark for including evidence)
3. E.g. They know what they are doing is wrong, so they are anxious to avoid criticism. *(1 mark)*
4. E.g. You shouldn't take advantage of someone's generosity because they might withdraw it, just as the lady does when she puts up her fence. *(1 mark for stating a sensible message from the poem, 1 mark for an explanation)*
5. <u>Falling</u> leaves spiral down,
   Nature <u>dying</u> all around.
   All the plants slowly <u>ageing</u>
   (or <u>aging</u>),
   Every year sees them <u>changing</u>.
   Animals start <u>readying</u> dens,
   <u>Hoping</u> for spring again.
   (1 mark for every 3 correct answers)
6. a) E.g. Mei put her feet up.
   b) E.g. Rohan's legs were shaking.
   (1 mark for each)
7. Any sensible lines of poetry.
   (1 mark for four lines of poetry about the discovery, 1 mark for using language that allows the reader to work out what the character is feeling from the way they are described.)

Workout 4 — pages 8-9

1. E.g. Clichés are overused, so they make your writing seem unoriginal. *(1 mark)*
2. a) E.g. freedom *(1 mark)*
   b) E.g. The narrator wants to go "where there are no footprints to follow", which suggests that they long to be outside exploring.
   (1 mark for finding a relevant quote, 1 mark for explaining how the quote supports your answer)
3. E.g. The short sentences create a sense of panic, reflecting how the narrator feels trapped in the classroom. *(1 mark)*
4. a) I'm <u>desperate</u> to go outside — it's such nice weather today!
   b) Efia is a <u>voluntary</u> marshal during running events.
   c) If I go on a run without a coat, it's <u>definitely</u> going to rain.
   (1 mark for each)
5. a) Any sensible answer.
   (1 mark for addressing the prompt, 1 mark for writing an introduction that grabs the reader's attention)
   b) Any sensible plan.
   (1 mark for structuring the story to create a particular atmosphere, 1 mark for structuring the story so it maintains the reader's interest)

Workout 5 — pages 10-11

1. This girl's book is about people's everyday lives 700 years ago. *(1 mark)*
2. affluent *(1 mark)*
3. E.g. The claim that he is "history's wealthiest person" is "much-disputed". *(1 mark)*
4. a) E.g. "Musa set off on a Hajj"
   b) E.g. "Musa lavished the locals with gold"
   c) E.g. "flaunting his fortune"
   (1 mark for each)

Answers

5. Historians know that the people of Mali traded metals like iron, copper and gold. Half of the gold in the Old World, an area that included Europe, Africa and Asia, came from just three Malian regions: Bambuk, Boure and Galam.
(1 mark for 3-4 commas added correctly, or 2 marks for all 5 commas added correctly)

6. Any sensible answer.
E.g. In 1327, Musa <u>relocated</u> his capital to Timbuktu, which <u>he had</u> conquered earlier. He spent <u>vast sums</u> of money on improving the city, adding <u>many</u> new buildings such as a <u>lavish</u> palace. Timbuktu was a <u>vibrant</u> city, where learning, trade and religion all <u>thrived</u>. <u>The city experienced some turmoil</u> in 1330 when it was captured, but Musa <u>soon regained control over it</u>.
(1 mark for making each sentence more formal)

Workout 6 — pages 12-13

1. adverb *(1 mark)*
2. E.g. The words "jigs to the jangle of bells" are repeated. This reflects the way Rollo constantly pesters the King by emphasising how often he dances around.
(1 mark for an example of repetition, 1 mark for explaining its effect)
3. a) E.g. Each stanza has a regular ABCB rhyme scheme.
   b) E.g. It gives the poem a light-hearted tone that reflects Rollo's own light-hearted nature.
   (1 mark for each)
4. a) The King doesn't like any of Rollo's jokes.
   b) Rollo hasn't got a chance (or 'has no chance') of getting away with that prank.
   (1 mark for each sentence)
5. Any sensible answer that fits the rhyme scheme and syllables given.
E.g. And banished the jester from town. *(1 mark)*

6. Any sensible answer.
(1 mark for every line of poetry that has 8 syllables and forms part of a rhyming couplet)

Workout 7 — pages 14-15

1. E.g. Language that appeals to the senses. *(1 mark)*
2. a) E.g. "the iron wheels, which heaved a grateful sigh"
   b) E.g. "like a shoal of fish being drawn into a net"
   c) "sudden silence"
   (1 mark for each)
3. E.g. Comparing the crowd of people to a shoal of fish emphasises how they move as one. *(1 mark)*
4. E.g. By comparing the train to a charging bull, the writer highlights how powerful the train is. *(1 mark)*
5. a) torpedoes
   b) crises
   c) fungi
   d) knives
   (1 mark for every 2 correct)
6. Any sensible answer.
E.g. She shovelled coal into the furnace, which blazed brightly. Then, she shovelled in some more, causing the furnace to roar angrily.
(1 mark for splitting the extract up into shorter sentences, 1 mark for changing words or phrases so that the extract is clearer)
7. Any sensible answer.
E.g. The train ground to a gentle halt and the passengers staggered onto the platform, bleary-eyed and groggy from the long journey. The driver was the last to emerge. Unlike the passengers, he jumped from the cab with a spring in his step.
(1 mark for making the first 2 sentences more interesting, 1 mark for making the last 2 sentences more interesting)

Workout 8 — pages 16-17

1. an idiom *(1 mark)*
2. E.g. The questions list qualities of a good TV show, so it makes the reader expect that this show will be good as well. *(1 mark)*
3. E.g. It creates humour because the show's title is 'The Splintered Arrow'. *(1 mark)*
4. E.g. Irony is used to mock the show's producers for being unable to create a good plot despite the large budget.
(1 mark for naming a technique, 1 mark for explaining its effect)
5. "I'm not concerned about <u>unflattering</u> reviews and idle gossip," Raven said in a recent interview, <u>referring</u> to whether or not negative press has affected his desire to continue filming the show. "If anything, I've become more <u>committed</u> to the story."
(1 mark for each)
6. a) E.g. You should absolutely watch this show — it's the best one that I've seen this year.
   b) E.g. I hated this TV show from the moment I saw the tacky set design and terrible costumes.
   (1 mark for each)
7. Any sensible review.
(1 mark for giving an opinion on the book, film or TV show, 1 mark for using persuasive language)

Workout 9 — pages 18-19

1. E.g. The way a character is presented. *(1 mark)*
2. a) E.g. She is rude and demanding.
   b) E.g. Joy tells the cashier that the service has been "abominable", even though the cashier is doing their job well. This shows that Joy is unnecessarily rude.
   (1 mark for each)
3. E.g. Professional. The cashier replies politely and calmly to Joy.
(1 mark for a description of the cashier's character, 1 mark for explaining your opinion)

Answers

4. a) Mum called to ask Asif and <u>me</u> to bring her back a bag of carrots.
   b) My friends and <u>I</u> weren't sure which aisle would stock marshmallows.
   c) The trolley's squeaky wheel kept making Natalie and <u>me</u> giggle.
   (1 mark for each)
5. a) Any sensible description. *(1 mark)*
   b) Any sensible lines.
   (1 mark for addressing the prompt, 1 mark for using dialogue, 1 mark for using stage directions to show the characters' traits)

Workout 10 — pages 20-21

1. E.g. voters *(1 mark)*
2. a) E.g. people who live in Bindley
   b) E.g. The writer refers to "our town", which suggests they are addressing people in Bindley.
   (1 mark for each)
3. a) E.g. They want to make the reader excited about the new library.
   b) E.g. Exclamation marks create an upbeat tone and suggest that the opening of the library is an event to look forward to.
   (1 mark for each)
4. a) My best friend Manali never leaves the local library <u>empty-handed</u>.
   b) I found a dusty crate of <u>thirty-five</u> books in the dingy cellar.
   c) The most <u>interesting-looking</u> book was always checked out.
   (1 mark for each)
5. Any sensible answers.
   (1 mark for each of the main paragraphs, 1 mark for an introduction and conclusion that link to the other paragraphs)

Workout 11 — pages 22-23

1. second-person *(1 mark)*
2. E.g. A farmer who has been doing their job for many years. *(1 mark)*
3. E.g. To replicate the narrator's accent and manner of speaking. *(1 mark)*
4. E.g. The narrator's tone is thoughtful. They gaze at the sea and wonder what the "restless tides" might bring them in the future.
   (1 mark for describing the narrator's tone, 1 mark for explaining your answer using evidence)
5. a) Two volunteers, Rob and Liz, will be leading the hike.
   b) Amina likes painting, the countryside, reading maps and fishing.
   (1 mark for each)
6. Any sensible answers.
   a) E.g. towering resolute
   (1 mark for both)
   b) E.g. like a the great tail of a sapphire dragon
   (1 mark)
7. Any sensible answer.
   (1 mark for describing the scene in the picture from the kayaker's perspective, 1 mark for using at least one of your answers to question 6, 1 mark for describing what you can see and how you feel)

Workout 12 — pages 24-25

1. who the narrator is *(1 mark)*
2. E.g. Mr. Pontellier is abrupt with his wife and does not like it when she disobeys him. He speaks to her "irritably" and moves with "impatience" when she refuses to come inside. This suggests that he doesn't like her disobeying him.
   (1 mark for describing Mr. Pontellier's attitude to Edna, 1 mark for supporting this with evidence)
3. E.g. It suggests that married women were expected to obey their husbands' commands. Edna would normally have "yielded to" her husband "unthinkingly". This suggests that women like Edna are so used to obeying their husbands that they do it automatically.
   (1 mark for explaining what the extract suggests life was like for married women, 1 mark for supporting this with evidence)
4. a) P
   b) A
   c) P
   (1 mark for each)
5. Edna falls in love with a man named Robert, who lives at the resort. — 2
   After he leaves, Léonce and Edna return to their home in New Orleans. — 4
   Edna and her husband Léonce are at a holiday resort with their sons. — 1
   Robert leaves for Mexico, realising their relationship can never be. — 3
   (1 mark for all correct)
6. Any sensible answer.
   (1 mark for writing from Edna's perspective, 1 mark for describing Edna's arrival home, 1 mark for using a flashback)

Spring Term

Workout 1 — pages 26-27

1. I love sitting <u>by</u> the Seine <u>with</u> a coffee, watching boats drift <u>along</u> the river. *(1 mark for all correct)*
2. E.g. The writer is enthusiastic about Paris and feels positively about the city. They describe the streets as "full of life and laughter". This suggests they enjoy being there.
   (1 mark for making a sensible point about the writer's attitude to Paris, 1 mark for explaining this using evidence)
3. E.g. The writer uses positive adjectives such as "divine", "illuminated" and "majestic" to present Paris as a beautiful city.
   (1 mark for saying how the writer gives you a sense of what Paris is like, 1 mark for using evidence)
4. a) I'd
   b) They'll
   c) would've
   (1 mark for each)
5. You should have ticked: The metro is the best way to travel — it's cheap, simple and reliable. *(1 mark)*

Answers

6. Any sensible article.
(1 mark for advising how to get there, 1 mark for advising what to do there, 1 mark for advising where to stay and eat)

Workout 2 — pages 28-29

1. E.g. Drawing a conclusion based on hints in a text *(1 mark)*
2. a) E.g. It is very quiet as there aren't many customers.
   b) E.g. The waitress is sitting very still.
   (1 mark for each)
3. E.g. The waitress and customer know each other. The waitress pours him a drink "Wordlessly", which suggests that she doesn't need to ask what he wants.
   (1 mark for making an inference about their relationship, 1 mark for supporting this inference with evidence from the text)
4. a) You should have ticked: The horserider — a stranger to the town — dismounted warily.
   b) Clouds of red dust — stirred up by the wind — filled the streets.
   (1 mark for each)
5. a) It had been a long day and the <u>sheriff</u> was tired. Arriving back in town, he tied up his horse and <u>entered</u> the jail. He <u>noticed</u> at once that something <u>wasn't</u> right. The door to the holding cell, which he had left firmly <u>shut</u>, was now ajar. There was an <u>eerie</u> silence. Then, he heard a noise.
   (1 mark for every 2 corrections)

b) Any sensible answer.
E.g. The sheriff heaved himself from his saddle, rubbing his bloodshot eyes. After tying up his horse, he ambled into the jail. Once inside, he immediately sensed something was amiss. Sure enough, the door to the holding cell, which he had left firmly closed, was ajar. All of a sudden, a deafening crash shattered the silence.
(1 mark for making the first 3 sentences more interesting, 1 mark for making the last 3 sentences more interesting)

Workout 3 — pages 30-31

1. E.g. Vote for me as your leader because <u>I am diligent, decisive and driven.</u> *(1 mark)*
2. E.g. She wants Americans to support British women's right to vote. *(1 mark)*
3. a) E.g. By asking a direct question, she is encouraging men to see her argument from her own perspective.
   b) E.g. The use of repetition makes her speech memorable and emphasises the many challenges that she has faced.
   (1 mark for each)
4. a) who
   b) which
   c) whom
   d) that
   (1 mark for each)
5. a) E.g. Florence Nightingale was a nurse and social reformer who lived during the Crimean War.
   b) E.g. She is inspirational because she achieved many things at a time when women were often discriminated against.
   (1 mark for each)
6. Any sensible answer.
   (1 mark for writing about how to give a good speech, 1 mark for using language features, such as second-person pronouns, to advise your friend)

Workout 4 — pages 32-33

1. A poem without regular rhyme or rhythm *(1 mark)*
2. a) B
   b) A
   (1 mark for both correct)
3. E.g. Poem A is written using a regular rhythm, whereas Poem B is written in free verse. *(1 mark)*
4. E.g. Poem A has a hopeful tone — a candle can make "the darkness sing", which is a positive image. Poem B is more sad in tone and describes the shadows which are "Lost forever" when darkness falls.
   (1 mark comparing the tone of the poems, 1 mark for including quotes from both poems)
5. Shadows form when a <u>solid</u> object (completely) or (partially) blocks the light. The <u>clearest</u> shadows (often) form when the light comes from a <u>single</u> point like the Sun or a lamp.
   (1 mark for all three adjectives, 1 mark for all three adverbs)
6. a) Any three descriptive words or phrases about sunlight
   (1 mark for 2 words or phrases, 2 marks for 3)
   b) Any sensible poem.
   (1 mark for following an ABAB rhyme scheme, 1 mark for using 8 syllables in each line, 1 mark for using a metaphor)

Workout 5 — pages 34-35

1. "It's a murder mystery party<u>,</u>" Sam said<u>,</u> "and you're invited<u>."</u>
   (1 mark for all punctuation correct)
2. E.g. Caitlyn seems suspicious as it is suggested she is on edge and has something to hide.
   (1 mark for giving your opinion, 1 mark for explaining your answer)
3. E.g. The story is dramatic. It ends abruptly with an unexplained "bloodcurdling scream", which creates a tense atmosphere.
   (1 mark for giving an opinion, 1 mark for using evidence to explain your answer)

Answers

4. a) The case remains open; the detective is pursuing a number of leads.
    b) The gardener and the housekeeper had an alibi; the others did not.
    c) Sergeant Spuds has a clear motive; Private Peeler's reasons are unclear.
    (1 mark for each)

5. a) Any sensible answer.
    E.g. In *A Study in Scarlet*, Sherlock Holmes compares the human mind to an attic. He says that his brain uses "a large assortment" of tools which are in "perfect order". This shows that Holmes is methodical.
    (1 mark for selecting one or more useful parts of the quotation, 1 mark for embedding quotations correctly)
    b) Any sensible answer.
    E.g. In *The Murders in the Rue Morgue*, Auguste Dupin, a detective, uses an analogy. Dupin says men often "wore windows in their bosoms." This suggests he knows what people are thinking from their behaviour.
    (1 mark for selecting one or more useful parts of the quotation, 1 mark for embedding quotations correctly)

Workout 6 — pages 36-37

1. Yours faithfully *(1 mark)*
2. a) E.g. Passionate
    "I urge you to reverse this decision"
    (1 mark for a suitable adjective and evidence)
    b) E.g. Frustrated
    "conditions for cyclists have rapidly deteriorated"
    (1 mark for a suitable adjective and evidence)
3. E.g. She could use a sympathetic tone. This could help the person she is addressing feel more positive about the housing development.
    (1 mark for suggesting an effective tone, 1 mark for explaining your answer)

4. a) Although there are many cyclists in Wisham, the roads have no cycle lanes.
    b) The housing estate will be built unless the council refuses to give permission.
    c) Mara will attend the protest because she wants to protect local cyclists.
    (1 mark for each)

5. Recent data puts the town's population at 12 000 and the new estate will provide housing for at least 600 more. With just a handful of shops, restaurants and other facilities, Wisham already lacks amenities. Increasing the population without developing more will worsen the problem greatly.
    (1 mark for every 3 correct)

6. Any sensible answer.
    E.g. Dear Ms Sebley,
    I am thoroughly relieved by your decision to build a new housing estate in Wisham. Speaking on behalf of the many people looking to buy a house in Wisham, thank you!
    (1 mark for making an appropriate point in favour of the housing estate, 1 mark for using an appropriate tone)

Workout 7 — pages 38-39

1. Any sensible answer.
    E.g. To tell the actors how to perform their lines. *(1 mark)*
2. E.g. The darkness creates a sense of uncertainty. The "violent wind" creates a sense of danger.
    (1 mark for each way that the staging creates a tense atmosphere)
3. E.g. His tone of voice could be relieved. He could show this emotion by relaxing his shoulders.
    (1 mark for giving a sensible tone of voice, 1 mark for describing his body language)
4. a) Nobody could find any way of saving those flowers.
    b) It may be time to move the plants into the greenhouse.
    (1 mark for each sentence)

5. a) Any sensible plan.
    (1 mark for planning each scene)
    b) Any sensible answer.
    (1 mark for each element of staging described)

Workout 8 — pages 40-41

1. E.g. I'm going to buy myself some suncream. *(1 mark)*
2. E.g. The headline uses dramatic words like "Battles", as well as alliteration in "Horrific Heatwave" to grab the reader's attention.
    (1 mark for each way the headline draws the reader's attention)
3. E.g. It uses dramatic images, such as "Train lines buckling", to shock the reader and make them curious to learn more.
    (1 mark for explaining why the opening paragraph makes the reader want to keep reading)
4. E.g. The map helps readers to easily see the extent of the weather warnings.
    (1 mark for identifying a layout feature, 1 mark for explaining its purpose)
5. a) In the summer, I like scuba diving, having picnics and playing sports.
    b) Although it was hot, Flo, who didn't feel the heat, was wearing a jumper.
    (1 mark for each sentence)
6. a) Any sensible answers.
    (1 mark for 2 points that agree with the statement)
    b) Any sensible answers.
    (1 mark for 2 points that disagree with the statement)
    c) Any sensible paragraph using a point from part a) or b).
    (1 mark for fully explaining your point, 1 mark for giving a piece of evidence to back up your point)

Workout 9 — pages 42-43

1. When one line of poem runs into the next without a pause. *(1 mark)*
2. E.g. The alliteration emphasises the delicate way the skull is being handled as it is so fragile. *(1 mark)*

Answers

3. E.g. Personification. It suggests that nature does not want to give up something that has been part of it for a long time.
   (1 mark for personification, 1 mark for explaining what it suggests)
4. E.g. In the metaphor "Ripping through the fabric of a millennium", the word "Ripping" suggests that unearthing the skeleton is an act of violence and is therefore wrong.
   (1 mark for a metaphor that supports the statement, 1 mark for explaining its effect)
5. In the late 8th century AD, the Vikings carried out their first raid on Britain. Arriving on fast-moving longships, they attacked the monastery of Lindisfarne in Northumberland, stealing various items and killing many monks. The first raid of many, it marked the start of Viking settlement in Britain. // For many decades, the Viking capital of England was York, then known as Jorvik. The Vikings may have chosen this location because of its strategic advantages. York was accessible from the coast and it was situated between two rivers, making it easy to defend. // In the 1970s, archaeologists discovered the remains of various Viking artefacts in an area of York called Coppergate. Extensive excavations revealed thousands of artefacts, from clothing and pottery to building materials and animal bones. These have allowed us to learn much more about how the Vikings lived.
   (1 mark for each paragraph break)
6. a) Any sensible description using interesting or unusual adjectives. E.g. a fragmented, soil-encrusted vase *(1 mark)*
    b) Any sensible simile describing the artefact or part of it. E.g. as fragile as a snowflake. *(1 mark)*
   c) Any four sensible lines of poetry about the artefact being discovered.
   (1 mark for addressing the prompt, 1 mark for using your answers to parts a) and b) in your answer)

Workout 10 — pages 44-45

1. You should have underlined: creaking, hidden, foggy, night
   (1 mark for most or all of the above)
2. a) ramshackle
    b) E.g. The house is covered in "mould and fungus" and is "broken in places".
   (1 mark for each)
3. E.g. The sentences, which are joined by semicolons, list aspects of the house. This emphasises the run-down state of the house.
   (1 mark for explaining how the sentences are structured, 1 mark for stating the effect on the reader)
4. a) The building's <u>columns</u> are <u>beginning</u> to crumble.
    b) The <u>campaigner</u> saved the <u>extraordinary</u> building.
   (1 mark for each)
5. Any sensible answer.
   E.g. Vast screens, like colourful scoreboards, hung above the bustling airport check-in desks. Below them, passengers and crew hurried about, each one in a rush to get to their destination.
   (1 mark for each sentence that successfully creates a hectic atmosphere)
6. Any sensible paragraph.
   (1 mark for describing a setting in detail, 1 mark for using interesting vocabulary, 1 mark for using interesting sentence structures)

Workout 11 — pages 46-47

1. You should have underlined: crashed, pattered *(1 mark for both)*
2. E.g. Alliteration. It emphasises that her achievement is particularly noteworthy.
   (1 mark for alliteration, 1 mark for explaining its effect)
3. E.g. The simile highlights the diversity of bathtubs available. *(1 mark)*
4. E.g. Using the present tense makes the reader feel like the interview is taking place as they read it. *(1 mark)*
5. a) Who's
    b) whose
    c) who's
   (1 mark for each)
6. E.g. Are you looking for a new hobby? Millions of people across the world say sailing is the perfect way to unwind.
   (1 mark for each persuasive technique)
7. Any sensible paragraph.
   (1 mark for some attempt at writing a persuasive paragraph using at least one persuasive technique or 2 marks for a strongly persuasive paragraph that uses a range of persuasive techniques)

Workout 12 — pages 48-49

1. E.g. 'Its' means 'belonging to it'. 'It's' means 'it is' or 'it has'. *(1 mark)*
2. "Like children fascinated by a new toy". E.g. This suggests that the crowd have a sense of childlike wonder at this new invention.
   (1 mark for the simile, 1 mark for saying what impression it gives)
3. E.g. The repeated 's' sound emphasises how quietly the balloon rises. *(1 mark)*
4. E.g. The reader is encouraged to agree with Étienne's view of himself as a risk-taking pioneer. *(1 mark)*
5. a) I had taken off.
    b) They had flown.
   (1 mark for each)
6. a) Any sensible hyperbole. E.g. The crowd contained the whole of France.
    b) Any sensible onomatopoeia. E.g. The wind whistled.
   (1 mark for each)
7. Any sensible paragraph.
   (1 mark for each technique)

Answers

Summer Term

Workout 1 — pages 50-51

1. The new dish <u>passed</u> the taste test — it had a positive <u>effect</u> on diners. *(1 mark for both)*

2. E.g. Text A is enthusiastic in tone, using adjectives like "sublime" to describe the food. This exaggerated language suggests that the reviewer thinks highly of the restaurant. *(1 mark for describing the tone of Text A and providing evidence, 1 mark for explaining it)*

3. E.g. The tone of Text B is neutral, as its purpose is to inform and give a balanced overview, whereas Text A gives a personal opinion. *(1 mark for how the tone differs, 1 mark for explaining why)*

4. Sue wants to <u>borrow</u> a cookbook from me (the one I <u>lent</u> you). She tried to <u>teach</u> me a new recipe but I had already <u>learnt</u> it. *(1 mark for each sentence)*

5. Are you celebrating a special occasion<u>?</u> Why not celebrate it with us<u>?</u> We offer private rooms for up to 70 guests<u>,</u> a bespoke menu and a complementary decorating service. Contact <u>our</u> <u>knowledgeable</u> team today. *(1 mark for every 2 corrections)*

6. E.g. 'The Flying Pufferfish' in Top Middleton was recently inspected by the council's food standards team. Since the team found that urgent improvement is required, a temporary closure of the venue was recommended. Therefore, customers should make alternative dining arrangements until the issue is resolved at the end of January. *(1 mark for using shorter sentences, 1 mark for using appropriate conjunctions)*

Workout 2 — pages 52-53

1. We <u>went</u> to swim, but the waves <u>were</u> too rough. *(1 mark for both)*

2. E.g. The sea "makes its moan". This suggests that it is unhappy and restless. *(1 mark)*

3. E.g. The use of enjambment reflects how the sea's thirst is never-ending and cannot be quenched. *(1 mark)*

4. E.g. The sea is presented more positively in the second stanza — the sea bed is said to contain "Sheer miracles of loveliness", which suggests it is home to great beauty. *(1 mark for how the sea is presented differently, 1 mark for an explanation that uses evidence from the text)*

5. a) biologists'
   b) children's
   (1 mark for each)

6. E.g. Located in the Pacific Ocean, the Mariana Trench <u>is</u> the <u>deepest</u> point of the world's oceans. At <u>a depth of almost</u> 11 km, it is <u>utterly</u> devoid of light. *(1 mark for correcting each sentence)*

7. Any sensible lines of poetry. *(1 mark for using the present tense, 1 mark for including two interesting adjectives, 1 mark for including a passive verb)*

Workout 3 — pages 54-55

1. When two contrasting ideas are used close together. *(1 mark)*

2. a) E.g. "a watchful eye that seldom seemed to look at anything"
   b) E.g. She is very observant but also discreet.
   (1 mark for each)

3. a) E.g. Capable. The writer says that she "did not often make mistakes against herself", which suggests that she acts carefully and efficiently. *(1 mark for a sensible adjective and evidence from the text, 1 mark for explaining it)*

4. a) <u>Until Dickens was four years old,</u> he lived in the city of Portsmouth.
   b) Dickens advocated for the poor <u>because they were often mistreated by the rich</u>.
   c) He was buried in Westminster Abbey <u>despite his request to be buried in Kent</u>.
   (1 mark for each)

5. E.g. Dickens's description of Madame Defarge's husband as "a bull-necked, martial-looking man" makes him seem intimidating. This language related to strength and aggression suggests he would not be easily beaten in a fight. *(1 mark for fully embedding the quote)*

6. E.g. The nobleman is presented as wealthy and smug. For example, he is "handsomely dressed" and "haughty." He has "a face like a fine mask" which suggests he hides his emotions. *(1 mark for each quote that is embedded and punctuated correctly)*

Workout 4 — pages 56-57

1. hyperbole *(1 mark)*

2. E.g. The conditions in the area are very different to the conditions the spy is used to living in. *(1 mark)*

3. E.g. The spy feels very lonely. *(1 mark)*

4. E.g. He feels nervous — his "palms still felt sweaty" despite the cold, which suggests he is sweating from anxiety rather than heat. *(1 mark for describing how he feels, 1 mark for supporting this with evidence)*

5. I often asked my grandma for advi<u>c</u>e. I had to practi<u>s</u>e every single day. In 1969, I received my pilot's licen<u>c</u>e. We devi<u>s</u>ed a shelter against the storm. The agency performs a vital servi<u>c</u>e. The spy convin<u>c</u>ed the other officer. *(1 mark for every 2 correct)*

6. a) Any sensible answers. *(1 mark for every two points)*

Answers

b) Any sensible answer.
(1 mark for clearly explaining your point, 1 mark for providing evidence for your point)

Workout 5 — pages 58-59

1. The main character *(1 mark)*
2. **a)** The text uses third-person narration. — B
   b) The text uses a metaphor. — A
   c) The protagonist came to the city with an aim. — A
   (1 mark for each)
3. E.g. The protagonist in Text A feels a sense of urgency, shown by the short final sentence "And soon." The protagonist of Text B feels uncertain; she is "suddenly unsure".
   (1 mark for how the protagonist of Text A feels with evidence, 1 mark for how the protagonist of Text B feels with evidence)
4. **a)** We had two options: stay and struggle or leave the city.
   b) There is one single mode of transport: a hoverbus.
   (1 mark for each)
5. Any sensible opening paragraph.
   (1 mark for using relevant details from the summary, 1 mark for an opening that successfully grabs the reader's attention)
6. Any sensible opening paragraph.
   (1 mark for creating a sense of mystery, 1 mark for including a secretive character, an urban setting and futuristic technology)

Workout 6 — pages 60-61

1. You should have circled: their
   You should have written: they're
   (1 mark)
2. **a)** E.g. The general public. The text refers to "your local red squirrel network" which sounds like it is aimed at people generally.
   (1 mark for stating the intended audience and explaining how you know)
   b) E.g. A persuasive tone. This is effective because it encourages people to take action to protect red squirrels.
   (1 mark for describing the tone, 1 mark for explaining why this is effective for the audience)
3. The writer uses words like "serious" to create a sense of urgency and highlight the severity of the problem.
   (1 mark for explaining how the writer uses language to emphasise the severity of the threat, 1 mark for using evidence from the text)
4. **a)** squirrel-friendly
   b) beautiful-looking
   c) sweet-tasting
   (1 mark for each)
5. **a)** Strategies must be put in place to protect these animals' habitats. — 3
   We don't often think about wildlife within cities. — 1
   However, birds, waterfowl and even some larger mammals live in cities. — 2
   Furthermore, gardeners should leave some wild areas for insects. — 4
   (1 mark)
   b) Any sensible conclusion.
   (1 mark for structuring your conclusion logically, 1 mark for summing up the article)

Workout 7 — pages 62-63

1. a verse in a poem *(1 mark)*
2. time *(1 mark)*
3. E.g. Positively. The idler is described as having a "happy life".
   (1 mark for stating that laziness is presented positively, 1 mark for using evidence)
4. E.g. Ambition is presented as meaningless. A rhetorical question asks if the reader is "the better" for their ambition when they die, suggesting that ambition is ultimately worthless.
   (1 mark for how the writer presents ambition, 1 mark for explaining your answer using evidence)
5. **a)** My n<u>ei</u>ghbour ach<u>ie</u>ved his life's ambition.
   b) My fr<u>ie</u>nd's goal is to live in a for<u>ei</u>gn country.
   (1 mark for each sentence)
6. **a)** E.g. The road is as potholed as Swiss cheese. *(1 mark)*
   b) Any sensible poem that uses the line openings.
   (1 mark for using sensory language, 1 mark for using onomatopoeia, 1 mark for using alliteration)

Workout 8 — pages 64-65

1. "It's not possible!" she exclaimed.
   (1 mark)
2. E.g. By starting the text with a one-word sentence. *(1 mark)*
3. E.g. The shift in focus allows the reader to see that the chaos is widespread and not limited to just one area. *(1 mark)*
4. E.g. The short sentences create tension by marking this day out as extraordinary.
   (1 mark)
5. **a)** My computer (which is now very old) runs incredibly slowly.
   b) Robots (both big and small ones) will be everywhere in the future.
   c) I need the internet to complete a task at school (a history essay).
   (1 mark for each)
6. **a)** Any sensible description of the new invention. *(1 mark)*
   b) Any sensible description of what goes wrong with the invention.
   (1 mark)
   c) Any sensible paragraph.
   (1 mark for structuring your paragraph to create suspense, 1 mark for using interesting vocabulary, 1 mark for using a range of language techniques)

Workout 9 — pages 66-67

1. E.g. To give the reader a good understanding of what the place is like. *(1 mark)*

Answers

2. Any sensible answer.
   E.g. The reader feels impressed as the adjectives "soaring", "towering" and "lofty" emphasise the striking height of the buildings.
   (1 mark for the effect on the reader, 1 mark for explaining how this is created)

3. Any sensible answer.
   E.g. By using repeated 's' and 'sh' sounds in the phrase "hushed havens of peace". *(1 mark)*

4. Any sensible answer.
   E.g. The writer's purpose is to inform people about Naqsh-e Jahan Square. This is seen in the writer's use of facts such as who built the square and when it was built.
   (1 mark for stating the writer's purpose, 1 mark for explaining it with evidence)

5. a) Abbas the Great named Isfahan the capital city.
   b) Today, the city is inhabited by almost 2 million people.
   (1 mark for each)

6. Isfahan, <u>which</u> is Iran<u>'</u>s third largest city, has a historic and <u>scenic</u> bridge across its main river. However<u>,</u> the river underneath the bridge often runs dry.
   (1 mark for every two corrections)

7. Any sensible answer.
   E.g. Chaharbagh, which means 'four gardens', is a long tree-lined avenue in central Isfahan that was built in 1596. The street is famous for its beauty. Many tourists and locals visit the street because it is a popular place for socialising. *(1 mark for a text that flows smoothly, 1 mark for reducing the amount of repetition)*

Workout 10 — pages 68-69

1. You should have circled: the props, the lighting, the set
   (1 mark for all)

2. a) mysterious *(1 mark)*
   b) Any sensible answer.
   E.g. The "candles go out" without explanation when the knight enters, creating an unsettling, mysterious atmosphere. *(1 mark)*

3. Any sensible answer.
   E.g. The knight is presented as a mysterious figure. He says he is "that which you fear most" and "that which you most need". This paradox suggests that the knight is a complex character.
   (1 mark for making a point about how the knight is presented, 1 mark for explaining it using evidence from the text)

4. a) monarch
   b) mischievous
   c) scholar
   (1 mark for each)

5. Any sensible opening scene.
   (1 mark for creating an appropriate atmosphere, 1 mark for basing it on the summary, 1 mark for correctly using stage directions, 1 mark for formatting the dialogue correctly)

Workout 11 — pages 70-71

1. Any sensible answer.
   E.g. So that the reader can see at a glance what each section is about. *(1 mark)*

2. Any sensible answer.
   E.g. To present lots of numerical data in a visual way. This allows the reader to easily compare the number of piranha swimmers with the national average.
   (1 mark for stating why the writer has chosen to include a diagram, 1 mark for explaining your answer)

3. Any sensible answer.
   E.g. The text is structured effectively. For example, the numbered list presents information in a logical order. To improve it, I would move the diagram closer to the relevant point. *(1 mark for stating whether the text is structured effectively, 1 mark for explaining the point or stating any reasonable change)*

4. a) Piranhas<u>,</u> a type of fish from South America<u>,</u> are classed as omnivores.
   b) Although they are famous for their sharp teeth<u>,</u> serious attacks are rare.
   (1 mark for each sentence)

5. a) Any sensible points arguing for or against keeping fish as pets.
   (1 mark for every two points)
   b) Any sensible paragraph.
   (1 mark for fully explaining the point, 1 mark for using evidence, 1 mark for including an opposing opinion and explaining why you disagree)

Workout 12 — pages 72-73

1. ridge / badge *(1 mark)*

2. E.g. Both poems use a metaphor to compare death to sleep. In 'Soldier Rest', the narrator tells the fallen soldier to "Sleep the sleep that knows not breaking".
   (1 mark for identifying the metaphor used in both poems, 1 mark for finding evidence in one poem to support your answer)

3. a) E.g. 'Soldier Rest' has a regular rhyme scheme, whereas 'Futility' uses mainly half rhymes.
   b) E.g. The irregular rhyme scheme and use of half rhymes creates a disjointed rhythm. This links to the unsettling mood of the poem as the narrator reflects on the soldier's death.
   (1 mark for each)

4. a) torren<u>t</u>ial
   b) finan<u>c</u>ial
   c) mar<u>t</u>ial
   (1 mark for each)

5. a) Any sensible answers.
   E.g. Bombs fell around us like <u>hailstones in a storm</u>,
   Like <u>a pack of wounded animals</u>, we crept forward,
   (1 mark for each)
   b) Any sensible answer.
   (1 mark for using at least one poetic technique, 1 mark for making the second line rhyme with 'cloak' and 'smoke')

Glossary

alliteration	When words that are close together start with the same sound. E.g. "a big blue bag"
cliché	An overused phrase or opinion. E.g. "Tomorrow is another day."
context	The background to a text which affects the way the text is understood.
figurative language	Language that is used in a non-literal way to create an effect, e.g. personification.
hyperbole	When exaggeration is used to have an effect on the reader.
idiom	A well-known expression that is figurative rather than literal, e.g. "over the moon".
imagery	Language that creates a picture in your mind, e.g. metaphors and similes.
inference	Reaching an idea or conclusion, based on evidence.
list of three	Using three words (often adjectives) or phrases together to create emphasis.
metaphor	A way of describing something by saying that it is something else.
mood	The general feel or atmosphere of a text, e.g. humorous, peaceful, fearful.
narrative	Writing that tells a story or describes an experience.
narrator	The voice or character speaking the words of the narrative.
onomatopoeia	A word that imitates the sound it describes, e.g. "crunch".
personification	Describing a non-living thing as if it's a person. E.g. "The moon smiled at us."
purpose	The reason someone writes a text, e.g. to persuade, to argue, to advise, to inform.
rhetorical question	A question that doesn't need an answer but is asked to emphasise a point.
rhyming couplet	A pair of rhyming lines that are next to each other.
rhythm	A pattern of sounds created by the arrangement of syllables.
simile	A way of describing something by saying it is like something else.
stage directions	Written instructions in a play that describe how the play should be performed.
stanza	A group of lines in a poem, also known as a verse.
structure	The order and arrangement of ideas in a text. E.g. How it begins, develops and ends.
theme	A recurring idea in a play, novel or poem.
tone	The feeling created by the language of a piece of writing, e.g. happy, sad, serious.

Score Sheet

Fill in the score sheet after you finish each workout.

Write your scores below to show how you've done.
Each workout is out of 12 marks.

	Autumn Term	Spring Term	Summer Term
Workout 1			
Workout 2			
Workout 3			
Workout 4			
Workout 5			
Workout 6			
Workout 7			
Workout 8			
Workout 9			
Workout 10			
Workout 11			
Workout 12			